T0302755

THE GHOSTS *of* AUTUMN

THE
GHOSTS *of*
AUTUMN

A SEASON OF HUNTING STORIES

JOEL SPRING

Skyhorse Publishing

Skyhorse Publishing books may be purchased in bulk at special discounts for sales promotion, corporate gifts, fund-raising, or educational purposes. Special editions can also be created to specifications. For details, contact the Special Sales Department, Skyhorse Publishing, 307 West 36th Street, 11th Floor, New York, NY 10018 or info@skyhorsepublishing.com.

Skyhorse® and Skyhorse Publishing® are registered trademarks of Skyhorse Publishing, Inc.®, a Delaware corporation.

Visit our website at www.skyhorsepublishing.com.

10 9 8 7 6 5 4 3 2

Library of Congress Cataloging-in-Publication Data is available on file.

Cover design by Tom Lau
Cover photo copyright Michael Ringer

Print ISBN: 978-1-5107-0482-4
Ebook ISBN: 978-1-5107-0483-1

Printed in the United States of America

CONTENTS

1

THE GHOSTS OF AUTUMN

IT HIT me as soon as I stepped out of the truck. The cold air gusting off Lake Ontario penetrated my lungs, causing an involuntary gasp before stinging my eyes and sending a chill not only through my body, but also into my soul. The warm September day, and the summer that had long since worn out its welcome in my world, suddenly melted away in the harsh and inviting arctic air. Turning into the wind, I faced the lake, welcoming the bracing cold as it washed over me. Summer slipped away as the gusts ushered in the first hints of autumn, if only for a little while.

Sitting on the tailgate with the old twenty-two rifle across my lap, I thought little of the squirrel hunting which I was allegedly here to do. I thought *nothing* of work. I thought nothing of stress. I was completely in the moment, something at which I've never been skilled. This is why hunting season brings me back every year. It's the opportunity to focus and the chance to just *be*.

Whispering on the north wind, the ghosts of autumn are everywhere. Their voices mix with the music from the first waves of geese coming in over the lake. The past is never far. To the south, Dad and I are hunting squirrels in the oak stand on the peninsula. To my west lie the backwaters of Twelve-Mile Creek where John and I are laughing and nearly capsizing the canoe due to carelessness, adventurousness, and just plain silliness. Ted is swimming in the murky water, happily retrieving the handful of ducks we somehow manage to hit, his great jaws clogged with feathers and duckweed. The fields to the east are full of ghosts and memories and the small victories of my dogs (and those of my friends) flushing woodcock and rabbits and pheasants and the occasional unlucky squirrel and fox, coyote and woodchuck. Mike, Maggie, Ted, Minnie, Jake, Charlie, Cagney . . . so many dogs that brightened our lives for such a short time. And now Max, my golden retriever, carries the weight of being endlessly compared to all the dogs that came before him. If you have the time, I can point you to a quiet stand of ash saplings where just two years ago Max flushed his first woodcock and made a proud stiff-legged retrieve. I could show you where he posed for a photo with a huge rooster pheasant in the shade of a red oak after a long chase across a grass field. It has become one of my favorite photos among the hundreds that grace the pages of a dozen old photo albums and several hard drives.

It's not only the ghosts that walk these fields, but also we, the living, that honor them. Perched on the tailgate, I try to remember all of the hunts over the years, but it is an impossible task. I struggle now to recall everyone I've brought here in my time to share in the places that have meant so much to me. I can't. Occasionally the memories will surface throughout the coming season. Many are gone though, lost forever on the cold breeze of time. That is as it should be. Nature is, if nothing else, always moving toward the next season. Fall never mourns for summer.

The woodcock migration is underway, as much a mystery as anything else a hunter may or may not know. That is, in and of itself, a lesson. We don't need to know everything. Why? Because we *can't*. We *shouldn't*. Soon the north wind will carry their secretive flight down from Canada. Not long after, the deer will begin their breeding season, another enigma of the outdoor experience that might have something to do with moon phases or temperature changes. Maybe it's just magic. In a few more weeks pheasant season will be here with its colorful birds and exciting chases through long-grass fields, brushy tangles, and thickets I've hunted a hundred times before with old dogs and old friends for more years than I can count. More than one *new* dog and *new* friend has been welcomed here as well. Chasing dogs through the rutted fields will bring me back to my youth while callously reminding me how long ago it was. It's been a lifetime, perhaps an eternity, not to put too fine a point on it. The length of time doesn't matter. The continuity from then to now is all that does. It's all that ever matters. The circle. The wheel of life. *Ka.* The twenty-five-year-old ghost of my younger self also walks with me. We have some spirited discussions from time to time. I'm older and wiser than he, but not nearly as much fun.

Before heading into the oaks to search for squirrels and look for other things I may not find, I meditate just a while longer. The fields and woods and old orchards here are sacred ground. I feel the presence of my old friends. I am humbled in the face of the beauty of this place, and experience the quiet only found in nature. The peace for which we all search envelops me. On my worst days I've never failed to find it here.

This is my cathedral. These are my meditations. I was raised Methodist, but this is my religion.

2

THE GHOSTS OF LASCAUX

THE STORY starts with four French boys and their dog walking in the woods on a fall day in 1940. Most of my favorite childhood memories start with a boy walking his dog in the woods on a fall day. In fact, a large percentage of my all-grown-up stories start with a fall day, a dog, and the outdoors. So, to this story, I can most definitely relate. The boys were reportedly searching for a mysterious tunnel they'd heard other locals talking about. That sounds like the start of a great adventure to me, and it certainly turned into one for them. Their dog, curiously named Robot, discovered the hole first, sniffing around the entrance to the hidden underground chamber. The boys, convinced they'd discovered the legendary tunnel and were mere inches from untold treasure and riches, did as most boys would do and slid down the small, steep tunnel into the uncertain darkness. Fortunately, their descent didn't end with a hundred-foot plummet or death at the bottom of a well, or an avalanche of suffocating soil or any of a hundred other horrible fates that may have awaited them below the earth's surface. Lucky for them, indeed. It soon became evident that it was very lucky for all of us.

The boys first found themselves in what would soon be called the Hall of Bulls. Googling the photos as I have many times during the writing of this segment, it is impossible to fully appreciate what the boys and their Robot saw. Some of the nine hundred animals painstakingly recreated on the walls of the Lascaux Cave are massive, life-size and then some. One particular bull in the Hall of Bulls is over fifteen feet long. That doesn't translate well to a twenty-inch computer monitor. Of the nine hundred animals, over six hundred have been positively identified as being species that shared the landscape with the ancient artists seventeen thousand years ago. These paintings were thousands of years old when the Egyptian architects had their first planning meeting in Giza to discuss the new blueprints for that little "pyramid project."

The discovery didn't only blow the minds of the young explorers. In a few short years Lascaux would effectively set the scientific world on its ear as well. Previously thought of as hulking brutes, our ancient ancestors were suddenly understood in an entirely new light in the hearts and minds of scientists and laymen alike. No longer looked upon as little more than primitive, apelike men (or manlike apes if you prefer) with only a passing resemblance to our modern culture, modern science suddenly realized that what we previously thought we knew about this ancient civilization was wrong. Very wrong.

Good going, boys (and Robot)!

The Cro-Magnon of the Upper Paleolithic was undeniably a wonderful artist. The artwork is detailed and colorful and represents, in some cases, some of the earliest forms of animation with the animals coming to life in bursts of speed and repetition. Picasso was an early visitor to the cave at Lascaux and remarked how man has learned nothing new in the past many thousands of years—higher praise for those apelike artists than one would expect from one of the greatest of our time.

Debates still rage decades later about the cave paintings. Did they represent many generations of cave dwellers, each adding their own artwork to the place? How did they light the dark cave to paint the artwork? Did they have the technology to erect the scaffolding that was certainly required to do some of the twenty-foot-high artwork adorning the ceiling? All are rational questions. There is one debate, though, that is universal. Lascaux and other famous caves such as those near Maros in Indonesia (dated to be more than thirty-five thousand years old), Chauvet (also in France), Altamira in Spain, and a host of others all beg the same question. That question, in every piece of literature I can get my hands on, is a very human question.

Why?

The experts weighing in on the *why* of the cave paintings include paleontologists, anthropologists, behaviorists, modern artists, and a bunch of other "-ists." It seems to me that the only people that haven't yet been invited to chime in with an opinion are today's closest descendants of the cave artists: us—modern hunters.

Paleolithic man had to hunt for food. Sure, you vegans, they *gathered* too if that makes you feel better. But plucking roots and berries is nowhere near the spiritual, communal, dangerous, exciting, and inspiring experience that hunting wild, warm-blooded beasts was and *is*. None of the Lascaux artwork, as far as I know, depicts berry picking.

What we now do with shotguns and compound bows and highly accurate rifles was then undertaken with spears at *get-to-know-you* range. And the game they pursued included ancestors of our still-lethal big cats, woolly mammoth, large forest bovines, bears, and an extinct deer wonderfully depicted at Lascaux known as *Megaloceros,* which in Greek means "big freaking deer." (It actually means "big horns," but with a deer that stands seven feet at the shoulders and whose antlers surpass twelve feet in width, that was in fact one *big freaking deer*.) If I'd been in the ancient woods and had managed to spear a *Megaloceros*—or at the very least managed to survive an encounter with one without being mercilessly impaled and carried away on those twelve-foot antlers—I'd want a reminder of the day. Taxidermy would be out of the question, as few good taxidermists were working during the Paleolithic. The ones that were undoubtedly commanded very high rates. Camera technology was a few thousand years away. What's the next best thing? Paint your depiction of the event on the cave wall, of course. Preserve the memory.

Simple.

Take a handful of red ochre, maybe a little iron oxide and manganese, and get to work. Ten years from now you can point to the painting and say, "Remember that day?" Your wife can say, "You're not going to tell the *Megaloceros* story again, are you?"

Little has changed in seventeen thousand years. Sitting here typing, I'm surrounded by memories of days afield. A few deer heads (none with a twelve-foot spread, unfortunately, though there's one that's *almost* two feet), a couple of bears, some deer skulls found on scouting expeditions, a mounted pheasant, and several dozen photographs adorn the room. Joy is a good sport about our cave decorations.

When I was a younger man with only a few taxidermy specimens on the wall, I used to horrify my non-hunting friends and family by calling it "The Room of Death." I was more prickly back then and only said it to people whose buttons I liked to push. It often worked. Many years later I now realize that it is, in reality, "The Room of Life." The photos represent a moment in time with a hawk at the birdfeeder, or a deer with a wonderful velvet rack glistening in the sun while standing in a wildflower field. The animal mounts represent moments in my life when my adrenaline never flowed harder, my heart never beat faster, my mind was never more inspired and focused by nature. If you come over sometime, I can tell you the story of each mount, right down to how the weather was that day. Remind me to tell you about almost sinking the jon boat trying to retrieve my first big Maine black bear. That story would make a wonderful cave painting—though I'm not sure which color best represents *fear*.

To me there is no *why?* for the Lascaux cave paintings.

Scientists try to put a label on them, as scientists are inclined to do. Was there religious significance? Were the hunts symbolic rituals? Rites of passage? Was painting simply a matter of recording some memories of days gone by or a particularly good hunt for *Megaloceros* venison? Is there a cultural meaning?

Yes, yes, yes, yes, and yes.

I'm sure of it. I am an expert in the field because I am frequently out in that field. Our own ideas of immortality are not new. In fact, they are as ancient as the Cro-Magnon genes that course through our modern blood. The ancient hunters painted those images to enjoy for themselves. They did it for their kids. They did it for us. They did it for those four young boys and their dog Robot to one day discover. They said, "We were here and this is what we cared about. This is what made us happy. This is how we lived. This is what rocked our world."

Lascaux simply says, "This is who we are."

They told their story directly and beautifully. Isn't that what we all want to do?

3

THE GHOSTS THAT
WALK WITH ME

THE GHOSTS that walk with me in those long-grass fields come and they go. No two memories are alike, just as no two days can be. I'm not a morose person by nature. I love life and I love to be in the moment, especially with soft earth under my feet and an expanse of outdoors in front of me. Living one moment at a time is not something at which I am skilled, but when I'm winding my way through some quiet, wild place, it comes as naturally as breathing. Some days there is little more on my mind than the happiness of watching Max and his boundless energy as we tear up the countryside on the trail of pheasants and woodcock and whatever else might cross our path. There are, however, two ghosts that always walk with me. In the fields, in my memories, in many waking moments, and very often in my dreams. Maggie and Ted are never far from my side. Though many years have mellowed my grief in the passing of the two best dogs that ever lived, their absence in the physical world has no bearing on their presence in my heart.

They are my constant companions.

If someone wanted to tailor a set of circumstances with the sole intention of breaking my heart, they couldn't have hatched a better plan. Several years have passed and I think it's now safe to say that I will never get over those two weeks. Since then, other dogs have come into my world, brightening my life in the way that only dogs can. Still, I miss Maggie and Ted with a depth of sadness and despair I didn't think possible under any circumstances, much less the death of a dog. I never understood people grieving deeply over the loss of a pet. After putting my two favorite companions and loyal friends into the ground with my own bare hands, I now understand.

This is part of what it is to love dogs.

As she had on a thousand hunting trips and a hundred other adventures, Maggie rode in the seat next to me. Instead of anxiously looking forward, panting eagerly with the anticipation of whatever the day might have to offer, she was curled in a small ball, head in my lap, quivering. The stench of urine filled the old truck in which she'd ridden to some of our most joyous days in the field. Occasionally looking up at me, her once bright eyes were clouded and sunken. She hadn't eaten in four days, soiling herself for half of that time. She had been shaking for the last twelve hours and I knew the end was near. My boss, an avid dog person with a house full of everything from pugs to St. Bernards, told me that I would know when it was time. I did and it was. The decision to have my best friend put down wasn't a hard one. Telling my young daughters was harder than making the call. The decision seemed like common sense. It seemed compassionate.

Until now, with my little dog on the seat next to me.

Now, nothing was clear. With my left hand I gripped the steering wheel hard, gritting my teeth. With my trembling right hand, I stroked Maggie's matted and stained fur. The early June sun pierced through the trees as I pulled down the long driveway leading to the vet's office. Once in the parking lot, I lifted Maggie out—her springer spaniel roundness now just a brown and white bag of fragile old bones. I talked to her on the way in and the way down the stairs to the office. Trailing a trickle of dog urine and a river of human tears, all semblance of dignity on both of our parts was gone. In the lobby, I put her on the ground and hugged her one last time. I'd called ahead. They were waiting for me when I finally went in.

The vet asked if I wanted to say goodbye.

He was an old school vet, and I liked him. He could be gruff and coarse at times and sometimes had more patience for his patients than their people, but underlying that was kind compassion and a love of dogs. That was plenty for me.

"I did," I managed to get out between silent sobs.

Did I want to be there for it?

"I don't think so."

He nodded, looking at me over his glasses, and told me that they could wrap her up for me after verifying that I was taking her home for burial. Fully unable to speak now, I just nodded and patted Maggie once on the head. My hand was barely under control, shaking horribly. My little bird dog didn't look at me as her head hung low across the vet's large forearms. She seemed to be fading right then and there. The light, what little was left, was going out of her eyes. I wondered if I should have waited another day.

No. That would have only been for me.

Looking into my red eyes one last time, the old country vet turned and went into his examination room. The receptionist asked for forty dollars. I wrote the check. The ordinary act of scratching my name and the numbers on the blank check helped me out of the numbness of the nightmarish day.

The period of time that passed probably should have felt like an eternity but the two or three minutes that elapsed just before the door reopened felt just like two or three minutes. Funny how things like that work. Time can compress and fold in on itself, passing like the wind. Sometimes an hour can seem like a lifetime. Sometimes, though, time is just time and a few minutes feel just like a few minutes.

When he emerged, the vet carried what looked like a small leaf bag. The thick plastic was in roughly the shape of my beloved little bird dog. *He put Maggie in a garbage bag.* It was the most horrible thing I've ever seen in my life. Time betrayed me, slowing down and elongating, stretching out impossibly far and moving forward almost imperceptibly.

He asked if I wanted him to carry her out.

I shook my head, my chest wracked with sobs that never quite made it to the surface. The vet put his hand on my shoulder and said something very kind. I don't remember what it was. Much like the words I whispered to Maggie on the way down the stairs, the words didn't matter. They were placeholders to fill in the spaces where words no longer meant anything.

Twice on the way home I put my hand on the bag on the seat next to me. Maggie's heat still radiated. Both times I recoiled as I felt the warm, familiar features of my dog under the thick plastic. Each time I touched the bag, I wanted to throw up. Reaching my house, I pulled the truck all the way down the driveway, around the pool, and into the backyard. Bouncing through a small drainage ditch I'd dug by hand when Maggie was just a nagging little puppy nipping at my heels in the piles of dirt, I pulled the truck up under a small grove of white pines, their long, soft needles creating an oasis of shade. I laid Maggie's bag there on the ground and went to the shed for the shovel.

The digging was horrible. Roots. Rocks. Pieces of metal and stone from the old barn that stood here a hundred years ago. I blasted through them with the point of the shovel, sometimes pulling at the roots with my bare hands. Digging slowly and thoughtfully at times, smashing and chopping furiously at others, I took my grief out on the earth. My muscles ached and my hands became blistered. My left thumb got punctured by an old piece of buried wire; blood streamed down my forearm. Still I dug, harder and faster and deeper. When the four-foot hole was finished, so was I. Lying back on the dirt pile, I looked at the sky, now graying in the west. Clouds raced, chasing away the blue. Rain was coming. I thought of other funerals. My great-grandmother. My grandmother. Cold. Rain. Disjointed images of sadness. A gray collage of heartache.

I carried Maggie across the yard to the small grave in the back corner. A rooster pheasant cackled in the field behind us, anticipating the storm. I don't know if I believe in signs but I took that as a sign. How many of those big old pheasants had Maggie flushed for me in that field? Dozens and dozens and dozens. Today the pheasants could celebrate, though their lives would be much less exciting now.

So would mine.

I lowered the bag into the ground. Looking into the hole, the ugly black plastic seemed wrong to me. I reached down and pulled a few holes in the bag, not looking down for fear I would see her clouded, lifeless eyes looking back at me through one of the tears. The pheasant cackled again, protesting the first few drops of rain. I began shoveling the pile of red dirt and clay over my old friend. By the time I was done the rain fell steadily and all that remained of my bird dog was a mound of fresh earth next to her favorite rabbit thicket.

Ted, my old black lab, stayed on the back deck the whole time I put his hunting partner into the ground. Charlie, the new springer pup, was tethered to a rope on the deck, protected as always by the watchful eye of his big black friend. I paused at the deck to tell Ted what happened. I put my nose into the long, soft fur between his ears. Many tears fell there. He seemed to understand, looking into my eyes as I backed away. Charlie absently chewed the end of a poplar twig in perpetual puppy happiness. When I let him (and his stick) into the house, Ted didn't follow. I called him but he put his head down, pretending not to hear me. Finally, I helped him to his feet with one hand on his collar and one under his broad chest. He moaned in pain.

"I'm sorry, Ted. I'm sorry."

He looked at me as if to say, "I'm sorry, too." Ted was more human than most people I know. In fact, there aren't too many people I wouldn't have traded for another year with Ted. Hell with that, I would have traded them all. He hobbled into the house, favoring his left front leg more than ever, laying down just inside the door with a whimper. Charlie curled up next to him and, for a moment, I wondered who was protecting whom.

Later, in the house, I talked to the kids. Jessica welled up with tears and hugged me, emotion pouring out of her. Jennifer went to her room to grieve alone. I could see both sides of me in both of their reactions. Their pain must have been immense, too. Maggie was a fixture in my life for only twelve years. She'd been with the girls for their whole lives. I had no words of comfort. I was too busy trying not to cry to do much of a job consoling anyone else.

If not the worst day of my life it remains in the top few. No. Strike that. It was *the worst day in my entire life*. The bottle of bourbon seemed like a good idea. Maybe the scotch in my desk drawer. Either way. Either one. Maybe both. Once the kids were out of earshot, I went into my basement office, put on some music, and drank and cried.

Finally finding sleep with my head down on my desk as I had a hundred times before, I awoke sometime in the middle of the night to find Ted on the couch opposite my desk, sleeping peacefully. He hadn't been able to make it down the stairs in a long while and I sighed, knowing I'd have to carry him back up. Still, I was glad he was there. Ted always made me smile. Just typing his name today, a decade later, makes me smile. Like most dogs, Ted had the uncanny sense to know how his people were feeling. Unlike some dogs and most people, he seemed to want to *do* something about it. He knew how I was feeling, and it must have been worth the pain of descending the stairs to come and watch over me while I slept off the booze. Ted the protector. As he slept, his feet twitched in concerted movements. He whimpered quietly in his dream, an excited cry, anticipating something superb. I imagined that he was chasing pheasants with Maggie running out ahead of him as she always had, breaking through the brush and long grass, his legs as strong and fast as they used to be and the golden fields full of bird scent. The thought comforted me. When he awoke, I struggled to get him back up the stairs, pausing once on the steps to rest with his great, fuzzy ninety-pound weight on my lap, my nose again full of his soft black fur. Had I known what the coming days had in store for both of us, I would never have left the basement.

"Yes, I see it."

Ted whimpered pitifully as the veterinarian rotated his left front leg outward. The bone tumor, over which I must have run my hand a thousand times in the last few weeks without notic-ing, was big and round and ugly. Only noticeable when his leg was twisted at this angle, it was as large as an orange. The vet shook his head and looked into my eyes.

This can't be happening.

A day earlier, just eight days after putting Maggie into the cold ground, Ted had fallen asleep on the living room couch. Knowing that he would have a hard time getting down, I placed his soft dog bed in front of the couch. When he finally awoke and slid off the couch onto the bed everyone in the house came running with his cry of pain. He lay whimpering and panting, holding his left leg at a strange angle. I held his head after he uncharacteristically snapped at me, leaving bite marks in my hand for the first time in his life. Maggie used to snap at me, sometimes drawing blood depending on her mood, but never Ted. Gentle Ted. Charlie and I stayed on the floor with him for most of the evening, leaving him only to bring a bowl of water, that he ignored, and some pain pills. He didn't move off the bed for the next twenty-four hours. I finally carried him outside the next morning but he lay motionless in the grass off the back deck, unable to support himself on his leg. I put him back on his bed and slid him back into the house. The kids asked a lot of questions, stroking his head and seeing into a future that I refused to accept.

The next morning, he whimpered like an injured puppy when I hoisted him into the truck for the ride to the vet. I didn't care what it took. Thousands of dollars in surgery, months of rehabilitation . . . whatever. I was not going to lose Ted. I hoped it was a sprain or a strain, or even a broken bone. *Anything*, just as long as the vet could fix it.

He couldn't. Of course he couldn't.

At the truck door, since I wouldn't put Ted through the pain of carrying him down the stairs to the office, the vet explained to me the ravages of bone cancer, and what we know of people who have suffered through it, wishing for death. This was an aggressive form, and my dog was obviously living in agony. The vet offered, suggested—almost *demanded*—euthanasia. *Now.*

"I can't do this again . . . not this soon."

He offered me some medication for Ted—very heavy medication—with the warning that I would be back in the next day, if not sooner.

I was only home with Ted for an hour before I knew the decision was the wrong one. His pain, even with the medication, was hell. He didn't deserve that. Through the back doors I could see Ted and Charlie lying in the sunny spot in the dining room. Even with the heavy sedative, Ted panted in pain. When the kids got home I told them. However saddened, they didn't seem shocked. I was the only one who didn't expect this. Denial isn't usually my way of handling things. Maybe I was turning over a new leaf.

I called the vet and scheduled an appointment for the morning. I gave Ted double the already heavy dose of the powerful medication and he finally slept. I hoped it wouldn't kill him. During darker moments I hoped it would. I lay on the bed next to him, feeling his heartbeat, listening as his heavy breathing slowed to a normal pace for the first time in many hours. I cried openly, already grieving for my old friend. Everyone in the house had somewhere else to be except Charlie. He stayed nearby. Springers are a wonderful breed.

Planning ahead this time, I dug Ted's grave while he and Charlie slept in the sunny spot by the back window. My hands, still blistered, ached with the effort. My heart ached even more. One of the kids let Charlie out the back door and he bounced around behind me while I started a new hole in the ground next to Maggie's. Every now and then one of the kids came to the back door to watch me dig. I covered the hole and the dirt pile with a blue tarp to protect it from another impending rainstorm.

Ted slept most of the evening as the rain fell outside. We took turns spending time with him. Even for a lab, he was special. His heart was as large as his big blocky head. Ted loved people, especially *his* people. Every now and then I glanced out in the backyard and caught a glimpse of that funereal tarp through the trees. Its horrible bright blue had no place against the shady green woods. I was glad when darkness fell completely and I could no longer see it.

In the morning the goodbyes were heartrending. Horrible. Jessica and Jennifer stroked his head and said their farewells, crying. I remembered a photo of the girls, both very young, with Ted still a lanky, crazy puppy. Not much larger than Charlie was now, he dutifully posed with Jess and Jen in front of the Christmas tree. It hurts to feel your heart break, but watching your child grieve enters another realm of sadness altogether. When the goodbyes were done I carried Ted to the truck. Thankfully, he didn't cry in pain as I put him in his bed on the tailgate. Then I climbed up to drag him into the bed of the truck. Sad, tired eyes ringed with gray looked up at me only briefly before I closed the cap. I called ahead to the vet and asked the receptionist to have him meet me in the parking lot. When I arrived the vet and receptionist came right out. I handed her the check. The vet commented sadly about the difficult week. *Difficult week. Yeah.* He said he'd been expecting me without so much as a hint of *I told you so* in his voice.

Donning his stethoscope, he listened to Ted's heart. Feeling gently along his front leg, his head shook almost imperceptibly when he felt the tumor again. I quietly wondered how many animals he had put down in his life. Hundreds? *Thousands*? He asked me if Ted was a hunter. I thought it was an odd question. *He was*, I said. He and Maggie were the best bird hunters I'd ever known. I told him that. The vet smiled.

"Ted is a gem."

He told me that he could see that. Picking up Ted's head, he looked into his eyes and smiled the saddest smile I've ever seen. There may have been tears in the vet's eyes. Many years removed, I'd like to think so.

"I'm ready," I said, not ready at all.

Hugging Ted's huge head, I looked away as the needle came out. I lost myself in that long, soft fur once again. Ted stiffened for a second, then relaxed. The vet took a step back and pocketed the syringe. The best black lab that ever lived sighed and slumped and I carefully let go of my grip around his neck. It was as if someone let the air out of him.

Is that it?

I gently lowered Ted's head to the dog bed. The vet offered me the stethoscope and I listened as Ted's powerful heart slowed and finally stopped. It was over in thirty seconds. I handed it back to the vet who listened for himself. Satisfied, he shook my hand and clapped me on the shoulder. No kind words this time. No words at all. They wouldn't have mattered, anyway. He sat on the tailgate of the truck for a few moments, watching as I wrapped Ted's lifeless body in an old pink blanket. *No plastic bag for Ted.*

The vet eventually walked away, head down, back into his office. Maybe he went inside and cried for Ted, too. I'd like to believe that. I closed the tailgate and took the short ride home, slowly and gently. Ted's last ride in the old hunting truck wasn't going to be rushed.

I still see that truck sometimes. The guy who bought it doesn't live far from my home and he frequently passes me on the road. Whenever I see it I don't think about family trips or hunting trips, fishing with the kids or other good things. I think about Maggie and Ted taking their final rides in that old pickup. I'm glad to be rid of it but wish I had sold it to someone further away.

I put Ted next to Maggie where he belonged. They had worked and played together, and together they had earned their rest. The hole I dug for Ted was deeper than Maggie's. I had to lie on my stomach in the dirt to gently lower him into the ground, still wrapped in the pink blanket. I strained against the weight, but managed to do it without unceremoniously dropping him or falling in myself. Covered in mud and brokenhearted, I sat alone in the back corner of the yard and oddly thought of my little sister. When I was young, my great-grandmother died.

She was a strong-willed, robust woman who lived around the corner from us on Estes Street. Julie, probably only six or seven years old at the time, loved her dearly. The night she died we were all at home, but Julie had been away for the afternoon for some reason and my mother had gone to pick her up. On the way home she told Julie of Grandma Nevin's death. I remember seeing the headlights through the rain running down the living room window when Mom and Julie pulled in the driveway. When the car doors opened a noise like I had never heard pierced November the night. Julie was *wailing*. I never heard anything like it before or since. Decades have passed and I still hear that sound in my head. The memory still tears at my heart.

That's what I wanted to do.

Kneeling in the dirt near my two dead dogs, I wanted to wail. I wanted to pound my fists like a child. I wanted to scream. Instead, I disappeared into myself. It was a long time before I came out and when I did I was not the same. Nothing was ever the same. The grief was a driving force in my life, a living thing. If you've felt that level of pain, you know. No matter the conventional wisdom, time does not heal all wounds. Sometimes you just need to learn to live with the wounds.

Jennifer, my artist, hand-painted the headstones. I picked up landscape rocks from Home Depot each time one of the pets passed on and she painted the names of the dogs and cats. For a long time I would cry when I mowed past the spot, going as fast as I could on the lawnmower as if to outrun the memory of that horrible ten-day stretch when I buried Maggie and Ted. Every now and then I'd discover where a pheasant had strutted across the graves, leaving their chicken-scratch tracks in the raw earth. This would make me smile but the smiles were few and far between.

Eventually, the small pet cemetery became a place of reflection. Only a few yards away from Ted's grave, a stray dog had once wandered into the yard when my girls were young and Ted was little more than a large puppy. From nowhere, Ted charged into the backyard, flattened the stray, and sent him packing. It was the first I ever saw of Ted the Protector. It wasn't the last time. Charlie and I used to go out there almost every day and look at the stones. *Maggie. Ted. Shadow. Ariel.*

I always wonder what dogs are thinking and I often wondered what Charlie thought as I stood weeping at the grave markers of my old friends. I think that what dogs think is not often what we think they should be thinking. For all their intellect, I don't think that they take time to reflect on death. Their lives are far too short to worry about it.

In that way, I think they are far superior to us.

It didn't take long before the woods tried to reclaim the weedy corner of the yard. I used to trim the grass and the brush back but I don't know if the stones are still there. I don't know if anyone looks over Maggie and Ted's resting spot and keeps the woods at bay, treating the spot as hallowed ground, a place to be protected from harm, as I used to.

I don't know if anyone takes Charlie out to the graves and tells him stories about Aunt Maggie and Uncle Ted. I hope so but I don't know.

I haven't been there in a long time.

4

THE GHOST IN THE MACHINE

MOST HARDCORE religions have some kind of rule about possessions. Sometimes, like the Amish, the rules are hard and fast, emphasis on the *hard*. Other religions are okay with possessions, though those same religions tend to frown upon idolatry. The religion of the fields and woods is different. Possessions aren't frowned upon. Instead, they are encouraged. Hoarding is sometimes the end result. It's probably not altogether healthy to have a thousand duck calls and two hundred and eighty shotguns. Having some *stuff* though, especially good stuff accumulated over time and imbued with meaning and soaked in good luck, is a universal truth among outdoorsmen. We all like stuff. Sometimes lots of stuff. Even the Amish appreciate a fine shotgun, from what I hear.

When it comes to guns, I truly don't care a whole lot about *fine* shotguns. I have friends who do. They're friends who have more money in guns than I do in my house and car, combined. But anything that costs more than my first car (itself an old clunker) is, to my way of thinking, keeping me that much further away from the savings that will be required to fund my next bear hunt. My current rotation of shotguns is on the surface remarkably bland and cheap. An old pump twelve-gauge that was poorly re-blued by a writer instead of a gunsmith is my go-to duck and goose gun and has killed its fair share of upland game as well. My number one shotgun is an old side-by that looks as if it fell into a wood chipper from which it was spit into a pool of battery acid. I have other shotguns—newer and shinier guns—but they rarely leave the safe. I'll probably end up selling them. That's what I did with my extra rifles. I have a rifle, and there were three in the safe not being used. I sold them.

The value of my duck gun doesn't mean much to me. In dollars, it's never been valuable. In memories, though, it is rich beyond belief. The fact that it was present during so many hunts, over so many years, over so many dogs, and has taken so many ducks and geese is enough. More than enough. The gun is beaten yet functional, ugly yet useful. It's a touchstone to other days and a bridge to today. It is one small way I can carry the ghosts of yesterday with me into the duck blinds and goose fields. I don't know how many muddy paw prints have been wiped from that gun, or how many times it was dropped into the Niagara River or Lake Ontario, but it doesn't matter. It is loaded with memories. Working the pump is like slipping on a soft slipper or sharing a hunting story with an old friend. It's smooth, quiet, effortless. No other duck gun ever feels right to me. I've given up trying anything else. Life is too short.

My rifle is a simple bolt-action model that's been manufactured in its current form for a long time. I've bought better guns, or what a gun collector might consider better guns, but it's never been replaced. The first thing I killed with it was my first big bear many years ago, and the last thing I killed with it was a big doe on opening day this year. The gun fits me. When

I pull the trigger it makes me a better shot than I am. But like my duck gun, what matters is that it's been witness to some of the best days of my life with some of the best friends I've ever had, and those memories live in the machinations of that simple design. It's a workhorse full of memories. Why shoot a big game animal with anything else? Why even ask?

My upland shotgun is an old side-by-side, one of the first new guns I ever purchased. When it became battered beyond recognition a decade and a half ago, I bought a semi-auto to replace it. I replaced that with an over-and-under the following year. I shot birds with both. I didn't bond with either. Neither seemed right, though the dogs didn't seem to mind as long as the pheasants fell to earth in a timely manner. After a couple of years of messing around, at one point even turning to my old duck gun for pheasants, I pulled the side-by back out of the safe and began putting more miles on it. I haven't stopped yet. Its stock bears the long, streaking scars from miles of brambles and thorns, brush and hardwood saplings. The bluing has held up surprisingly well, but the wood has worn down from the constant abrasion of the uplands. At some point during the mid-'90s I refinished it. It took only one season of woodcock and pheasant hunting to return it to its original abused patina. That is how it looks today. That is the gun that killed birds over every dog I've had. Innumerable pheasants have fallen at the end of its barrel, along with a few less woodcock and dozens of rabbits. Two very unlucky turkeys also made their way into the freezer over the old, worn bead of those double-barrels over the years. The shotgun has become such a part of me that I no longer think when I pick it up to shoot. I no longer point. I don't calculate leads. I never worry about following through. It's the only shotgun I've ever owned that, when a pheasant flushes, I entertain a fair degree of certainty that it will fall. The misses come but they aren't a result of the gun's lack of magic but, rather, a momentary lack of my own belief. Maybe the sun was wrong or the wind wasn't right (I know all the excuses). I've always been an average wing shot, but because of that shotgun I've gotten a better reputation than I deserve.

When I'm walking back to the truck with a tired Max after a long afternoon of tearing through the uplands, I sometimes look over the gun and focus on the scratches and think of the miles that put them there. Miles behind Maggie and Ted and Charlie and so many other friends, both here and gone.

The old shotgun has outlived many pairs of good hunting boots.

There are many possessions I've let go over the years but that shotgun will never join their ranks. I will be chasing birds with it as long as I'm capable of hobbling through a long-grass field and, once I'm gone, I hope it will be killing birds over one of my nephews for many years to come. I hope they feel the power coursing through that simple side-by-side shotgun. That *magic*. All of those ghosts in that simple machine. They're there, just waiting to be awakened. Each fall I am happy to open the door to the gun safe and let them out.

I have other possessions, of course. Being a big-game hunt-er who delights in wandering far into the wilderness, I have a pack full of stuff. Jammed full. When deer season is upon us, I spend two or three nights going through the pack. I replenish the toilet paper that can be used for marking blood (though that is not its ultimate or most frequent use), stoke the GPS with fresh batteries, and check the sharpness of the two knives that I'm quite sure I sharpened before I stored them for the off-season. I still check them. One of the knives is a utilitarian skinning knife that is an exact copy of one I lost many years ago during a deer hunt due to a carelessly unzipped jacket pocket. The other is a long-bladed Buck knife that is newer but also an exact copy of a knife I broke while trying to split the hindquarters of a deer a few years ago. Two knives. Why? Because I can. The other stuff in the bag all needs to be checked as well. First aid pack, survival blanket, a flashlight, compass, the GPS, extra batteries, a Zippo lighter, and so on. Depending on the season, there are bow parts, scope batteries, muzzleloader tools, a couple of pens (neither of which will write when it comes to filling out a deer tag on a frigid December morning in the mountains). There are light gloves and heavy gloves and extra light gloves and extra heavy gloves. At least one pair of fresh socks rests at the bottom of the pack, and a hat or three. There's string, rope, and other stuff that would make an Eagle Scout envious. There are a handful of ideas I've usurped from other guys with whom I've hunted, including an ingenious device designed to pull the butt out of a deer. Imagine my embarrassment the first time I used it and my deer was so small that it didn't fit. True story. I wasn't joking about the Eagle Scout, either. He borrowed the butt-puller. His deer was large enough that it worked wonderfully.

I sift through the contents, laying it all neatly out on the floor in front of the fire, and replace what needs replacing. Sometimes, I just play around with the contents and think forward to the season ahead. Gene Hill, one of my favorite writers, called this "Equipment Time." My wife sometimes calls it "Boys and Their Toys." Both are apt descriptions.

In the autumn of 1991, a very well preserved mummy was discovered high on a lonely mountain in the Ötztal Alps between Austria and Italy. The finding was significant from a scientific perspective not only because it was one of the only intact remnants of our ancient European ancestors, but because the boy was found with his toys.

Along with his clothes (which consisted of a leather hat, waterproof boots, and other articles less interesting to an outdoorsman) was his *stuff*. Ötzi, as he was nicknamed, carried all kinds of outdoor gear. A belt pouch contained a fire-starting kit with a small container of embers wrapped in maple leaves (complete with flint and tinder fungus), a scraper, and an awl. Along with that, he carried a copper ax, a bow, arrows, baskets, berries, and a flint-bladed knife. Ötzi carried a lot of stuff, and that was without Cabela's online catalog! Five thousand years ago I can only imagine that those early hunters also reveled in Equipment Time.

In a strange footnote, scientists very recently discovered through an MRI that Ötzi had been murdered. The lethal arrowhead lodged deep in his back had been missed in previous x-rays, but the MRI was clear as day, showing the point embedded deep in his boiler room. I can only presume he homed in on someone else's patch of deer woods or missed the "No Trespassing" signs that the neighboring clan had up. Stiff penalties in those days, I guess. It wasn't as if you could easily call the game warden. Even more interesting is that whoever murdered him didn't make off with Ötzi's stuff. This just leads me to believe that their stuff was probably better and his, not worth stealing. Maybe he was carrying around some broken-down old gear just because it reminded him of his dog.

You never know.

5

THE FIRSTS

THE FIRST squirrel of the year was a rather tame affair as hunting adventures go. Sitting in a sprawling grove of mature oaks, I basked in the cool September air, deceptively chilled by Lake Ontario; it was fifteen degrees warmer at my house only ten miles to the south. The cold lake winds are one of the things that entice me back to this place year after year. Unlike the fields to the north during the October pheasant season and the often-crowded creek to the west during the salmon and steelhead runs, I never see anyone here. That's the way I like it.

Kicking a patch of leaves clean at the base of a young beech tree, exposing bare earth to mute my shifting and squirming, I had only just settled in when the first squirrel raced up a giant white oak stretching seventy feet above me. I followed him in the scope but, just as I squeezed the trigger, he disappeared into a previously unseen hole high in the woodwork. Letting out a sigh, I was disappointed my first game animal of the year was going to be taken a mere five minutes into the hunt yet was snatched away just as quickly. Scurrying movement to my left revealed another large gray hopping across a log. I found him in the crosshairs and, when the little rifle cracked, he tipped off the back of the log. Success.

First squirrel of the year.

It doesn't have the same ring to it as *first woodcock of the year,* or *first pheasant of the year,* or *first big buck in a long damned time,* but it's a first just the same. It's a portal opening into this new and hopeful season. Firsts, not only firsts-of-the-season, are always a very spiritual aspect of hunting. They're reminders, welcome mats, optimistic hints into the rest of the season. I know, it's only a squirrel. But then, it's not. It's also a reminder of all of those other firsts. It is an integral part of the meditation and an invitation to remember different firsts and other small victories. These are the things that fill an outdoorsman's dreams especially in the long off-season. Going about the business of skinning the small animal before packing him away into my daypack and trying to find my first *second* squirrel of the season, I thought of my other firsts.

First things first.

I jumped headlong into hunting later than most, in my early twenties. The first animal whose fate I decided was a small button buck. I was in the wrong place at the wrong time, with the wrong clothes, with the wrong wind, and used tactics that could only be considered extraordinarily *wrong.* Leaving my stand after seeing the small deer feeding under an apple tree for the better part of an hour (maybe it was only five minutes), I impatiently climbed down and crawled toward the tree. Ten yards from the deer, keeping a bush between us, I reared up (completely shocking the animal) and arrowed him. He took two steps and fell over dead, his pyloric artery severed by the broad head as neatly as if by surgery. The fact that that wasn't the place I was aiming did nothing to change my elation. The effect was the intended one. I then realized that I had no idea what to do with a deer on the ground. A friend, who I'd go on to share many hunting and fishing trips for several decades after, came to show me the way. Every time I show some new hunter how to field dress a deer, I think about that day. In my jeans, t-shirt, and blood-soaked white sneakers (yes, you read that right), I learned how to remove the plumbing from a big-game animal (and I use the term *big game* loosely for that first button buck) while leaving all of your fingers intact. I haven't quite mastered the last part yet, and during Equipment Time I always make sure that my pack is loaded with not only bandages but gauze and duct tape as well. Pre-planning has served me well when it comes to self-mutilation and the patching often required to slow the flow of my own blood.

My first woodcock was killed over my longtime hunting partner John's black lab, Mike. Mike flushed a bird in front of me and I shot it while it was still near the barrels of my twelve-gauge. Did I hit it? Miraculously, *yes.* And *unfortunately,* yes. Woodcock aren't much of a meal to start with. What was left of that one would be hard-pressed to fill a young-of-the-year field mouse. But I remember that day very well, down to the last details. I remember the dog. I remember the blue sky. I remember to avoid shooting birds too close to the gun and, most importantly, I remember my *first.*

My first bear taught me many things. After a week of hunting a place that was guaranteed to have bears, I'd seen nothing. On the sixth and final night I changed my approach to the stand, thinking that perhaps the bear had been watching me walk in while silhouetted against a high ridge. For my last hunt, I put a sneak on below the ridge and through a small swampy drainage and settled in. Counting down the last few minutes of daylight on the last day of a long, bug-filled hunt with temperatures that were nearly too hot to endure, I almost gasped when the bear materialized at the edge of the long wood ferns only twenty paces from my ground, blind and at eye level. I don't remember shooting him. I don't remember the click of the safety or the roar of the rifle, but the bear cartwheeled and let out a roar that I can still hear twenty-five years later. Unfortunately, he took off into the darkening woods. My friend and guide, Ken Reed, who'd patiently taught me to field dress that first button buck, told me to stay put if I shot one. That was my first guided hunt. I didn't realize this was a hard-and-fast rule with most hunts but particularly during bear hunts. Being young, full of adrenaline from my first close encounter with a black bear, young, stupid, and *young*, I set out after the bear, convinced I'd made a good shot. By the time I fished my flashlight out of my pack with hands shaking as if they'd been dipped in ice all day and headed off into the fern-choked woods, the gloom had gathered into the gray-black shadow of mountain twilight. Complete darkness was not far behind. Going after that bear in the long ferns, I wasn't afraid.

Until I stepped on him.

The moan he let out was just a biological function of me stepping squarely on his lungs and the air escaping through his windpipe one last time. I nearly had my own biological function in my camouflage pants before realizing that the bear, which I'd distanced myself from in a series of acrobatic backward leaps, was indeed dead. The idea that I could have shot him again if he *wasn't* isn't even plausible. I was wrecked. Shaking. Exhilarated. It was well after dark before I'd calmed down enough to begin the field dressing. I didn't cut myself. That time.

The memory is as fresh as it was a quarter century ago. That's one of the best things about firsts.

There were first pheasants and first ducks and first dogs and first rabbits. I clearly remember shooting my first rabbit over my first bird dog. At the time I hadn't read up on how things were *supposed* to be and didn't realize that "running fur" was a

phrase used distastefully for dogs (and presumably their uneducated owners) that were allowed to chase rabbits. The first
time I took some other guys hunting and had the phrase thrown
in my direction I'm sure I said, "Yep, she is *great* at running
fur, isn't she?" I didn't know. The dog sure as hell didn't know
that she was not supposed to flush rabbits. We never stopped.
I've since read Charles Fergus's book *A Rough Shooting Dog*,
which seemed to agree with my propensity to let my dogs (all
of them—every damned one of them) hunt rabbits. Fergus's
book is the only book that agrees with me, but that's okay.

It must be true. He's a writer . . .

My first duck hunt on the Upper Niagara River ("Upper"
meaning *above Niagara Falls)* in January was another unfor-
gettable first. I'd duck hunted many times prior. No firsts there.
I'd never been duck hunting with (or even talked to) the two
guys with whom I shared the huge, spectacular duck boat.
They were friends of a friend and invited me to come along.
In the 4:00-a.m. darkness we stopped at a spot in the river far
from shore and very near the sprawling Grand Island bridges
and the boat pilot, Joe, simply said, "Here's where we get
out." When he dropped the anchor, I realized he was serious.
I really didn't know these guys. Had someone put a hit out on
me and it was time to go sleep with the fishes? Just as a pre-
caution I let them go in first. At the time, I didn't know there
was a grass island out in the river that was *only* waist deep in
places (and chest deep in others), surrounded by faster and
much more dangerous water. As we set the decoys in the dark,
I was more than aware of the plume of mist from Niagara
Falls. In the dark, at least, it looked dangerously close. Just
before sunrise the ducks started flying and some of the most
incredibly fast duck shooting of my entire life began as wave
after wave of mallards and bluebills presented themselves.
Halfway through the morning, the boat was stacked full of

birds. Three limits for three guys. I almost forgot that I was frozen half to death.

Moving slowly through the woods to another grove of even larger and more ancient oaks, I kept my eyes skyward, looking for the telltale shaking of the high clumps of still-green leaves. Farther down on the peninsula, John and I had our very first hunt together decades ago. He took a fat squirrel with his twenty-two magnum while I missed one with my shotgun. The plummeting squirrel nearly landed on my head and started what would over the years be one of many laughing fits that John and I enjoyed while hunting and fishing together. My dad and I also enjoyed our first hunt here together many years ago. He'd stopped hunting long before and this was the place that brought him back around. Next year I'll be taking my nephew and my young cousin here for their very first hunts—hunts that I hope will live with them long after.

So many firsts and so many more to come. God willing.

Not all of the ghosts of autumn are friendly and welcoming, but stalking through the hardwoods the memories were as light as the birds flitting through the oak branches above me, busy with the business of living. Ahead of me, another squirrel hurried across the obscure tractor path long overgrown by saplings. Sitting quietly in the leaves and dried acorns, I waited.

6

THE LESSER GHOSTS
OF AUTUMN

OCTOBER ISN'T always about deep blue skies and flaming red maples and yellow poplars that burn like torches, lighting the way to winter. Sometimes it's about green grass that has been tipped brown by the first hard frost, and the muted grays of the underbrush in a bird thicket. It's very often about cloudy, black-ish skies that in a few more weeks will usher in the first faint snowflakes. October isn't always showy like a bright rooster pheasant above a golden field. Sometimes, it's subtle and sol-emn like a woodcock hiding in the leaves that quietly welcomes the hunter into its reverent state of grace. Sometimes, it rains. The best fall days in my memory are often wet ones. The dogs work better. The birds hold tighter and flush closer and the wet blanket of woods and thicket make your solitude that much more real as the walls of nature press in even closer around you. I long for days like these and it's fitting that the woodcock opener is a wet one.

It was Max's first day (another first) of his third season and he'd long known what the gun coming out of the safe and the brush pants pulled from the closet meant for him. *Bird hunting.* He has a peculiar habit unlike any bird dog I've known of, curling up on the backseat of the truck into a small ball, staying that way until we arrive at our destination. Every other dog I've had has paced, whined, cried, panted, barked, and made a nuisance of themselves when they know we're on our way to a bird field. Not Max. He remained motionless in the backseat until we arrived at the woodcock cover and I opened the door. He was out like a shot, from zero to one-fifty in two seconds. Cutting tight circles around me while I suited and loaded up, bucking like a wild horse, he had energy to burn. His happiness was a joyous sight, even in those rainy and somber woods.

Coursing ahead of me in the long switchgrass, he seemed to know that we weren't hunting pheasants and were, instead, headed to the far northwest corner of the field where a stand of saplings always produced a timberdoodle or two. During his first year, for all practical purposes still a pup, Max flushed and retrieved his first woodcock in that small wood lot. He remembers that. Last year he also flushed a handful of birds there. It doesn't look like classic woodcock cover, but it has held them for as long as I can remember. It's a place where I've taken more woodcock over more dogs than any other piece of land to which I could point. I've come to believe that's because it is one of the first stands of saplings available when the birds make the long flight across Lake Ontario, and they fly in there to take a break after crossing the big lake. It's just a theory and anyone will tell you I am chock full of those. The poplar stand has never produced more than two woodcock at a time, but it tends to *always* produce at least one *every time.* And that's good enough for me, and plenty good enough for Max.

Following Max into the thicket, my brush pants already wet from the long grass, we'd no sooner stepped into the wet saplings when the unmistakable *peep-peep-peep* and fluttering whoosh of a flushing woodcock pierced the quiet woods. I jerked the double up to my shoulder, thumbing the safety and waiting for the bird to clear the brush. There was nothing but a quick blur as the bird slipped out the opposite side of the thicket. I put a shot after the woodcock as quickly as I could. Unfortunately, *after the bird* was exactly where it hit. Max, who'd been right on top of it before it flushed, looked for the downed bird that he'd never find before bouncing back to me, ears alert and brow furrowed. I've seen the look before.

Don't even tell me you missed.

I told him. He took it well.

That was the only bird in Max's favorite poplar stand. We trudged across the field to our next piece of bird cover. A hen pheasant went up in the long grass in between and brought a smile to my face as Max raced after her, undoubtedly certain that I'd lost my mind in first missing the woodcock and purposefully not shooting at a pheasant. I explained to him that pheasant season didn't start for another three weeks.

He didn't that take so well.

The next stand was a mix of maple and ash near an old irrigation pond. Several small ditches, now choked with saplings, showed bare ground littered with a great number of tiny, white woodcock droppings—white paint spatters against the dark earth. Max worked the area, snuffing and snorting and moving along at a slow pace, occasionally darting back and forth as he unraveled the ground scent of a bird's trail. After all these years, it still fascinates me just as much to watch a bird dog unravel a scent trail. Backward, forward, and side to side until it has determined (quite remarkably) which direction the bird is heading. Then it's off to the races.

Today was no different.

Once on the scent, Max made a quick dash up one of the narrow ditches with his nose never more than an inch off the ground, working furiously. Suddenly swerving hard to the left, he pounced and the bird went up. This time I was ready as it made a high, fluttering arc up and out of the cover, towering above us for a moment before toppling to the ground twenty yards away at the boom of the gun.

When it works, it all seems so easy.

Uncharacteristically, my golden boy didn't race for the retrieve, but rather kept working the ground in the area from which the woodcock had flushed. I urged him on to the other side of the thicket to pick up the bird, but he was locked in the area.

"We got him, Max. Fetch."

As it was early in the season, and I was a little rusty on the rules, I violated one of the few rules that I bother obeying when it comes to bird hunting: *Trust the dog.* As I turned my back on Max to start toward the downed bird, he flushed a second woodcock. I heard it at the last second and pivoted around in time to nearly get a face full of timberdoodle, and then spun back around for the shot. Naturally it was a miss, which is somewhat disheartening considering I could've caught the bird in my hat.

Certain the area was now officially cleared of woodcock, Max retrieved the first bird as if he had planned on it all along. A tiny game bird to start with, a wet woodcock somehow manages to appear even smaller. And in the jaws of a big bird dog, smaller yet. Max, familiar with my annoying habit of field photography, posed patiently before heading back into the subdued browns and greens of the damp thicket. Rain gently dappled the branches around us. A light fog rolled in as we moved to the next cover, wet and full of hope.

7

THE COLLECTING

OTHER THAN the taxidermy and photography adorning my modern Lascaux, I have a lot of what can only be loosely described as *outdoor stuff* and a lot of that is made of bone. There are deer antlers and moose antlers, bear skulls and coyote teeth. There are pheasant feathers and a black squirrel tail, some twisted corkscrew willow branches standing in a corner, there only because they are interesting.

Outdoor people are—almost without exception, in my experience—collectors. I've been collecting outdoor items since long before I hunted. I still have a shed deer antler from the late '70s, found in a cornfield and given to me by my cousin Debbie. She's still one of my favorite cousins. I've picked fossils from creek beds when I should have been focusing on the trout fishing. I've been collecting as long as I've been able to bend over and stuff something into my pocket or backpack.

Near my fireplace there's a skull from a whitetail buck that has been the subject of many hundreds of my photographs. I'm sure there's a photo of him framed somewhere in the house. A true monster of a ten-pointer and every bit of his 250 pounds, he lived in a place where hunting was not allowed and very few people have access. I was lucky enough over the years to locate a couple of his tremendous antlers. On my last shed-hunting trip, I found him—what was left of him, anyway—after having been pulled down by the pack of coyotes who keep in check the herd of deer that otherwise would overrun the area. If I could have hunted him I would have and I didn't begrudge the coyotes their meal. *Bastards.*

Maybe there's a small grudge.

Near that is the skull from my first bear, the sole reminder of him since I sold the rug several years ago. I don't need the skull. Hell, I didn't need the rug. I can still remember the way the air left the woods when he stepped out of the ferns. I can easily recall the exhilaration and the elation. Still, it was a nice reminder to have. Now that fur, black as midnight, lives only in my dreams. He was a small bear but he was mine, as much as a bear can be yours. The skull is a simple reminder, a concrete tribute to the bear that would become the first of many.

My dad is an avid collector—much more avid a collector than a hunter. Because of his collecting, I have other exotic things I wouldn't otherwise display on the walls of the cave. There are old, carved duck decoys, a pair of world-class caribou antlers, a rack from a small bull moose that he'd convinced himself was the rack from the world's largest whitetail deer. It still makes me laugh.

Every now and then over the years I've scaled the collection back. I've sold a couple of bear heads, boxes full of small antlers from deer I've killed, and a full coyote mount from a very exciting and fearful close encounter. Each and every time I've lived to regret those choices. From time to time, other than my cherished trophies, I have convinced myself that I don't need to be nature's garbage picker, not much different from the guy who drives around my block every Wednesday night in his small red Nissan pickup, hoping to find scrap metal in everyone's garbage. I've occasionally realized that I don't have to pick up every raccoon skull and owl pellet and heron feather and deer scapula and any other interesting thing that I find in the woods and fields and bring it home with me. The feeling doesn't last long; when it passes, I go back to those spots and hope they are still there. My room has several items that I didn't initially pick up . . . but then I did.

The need to collect and gather and display is as ingrained in me now as it was when I was a young boy walking those same fields, collecting bird nests and anything else I could get my hands on. My collector's nature often comes out in my photography; it is, I suppose, the same need. Writing, too. It's all the same drive. I take photos because I want reminders and I want some proof of what I was doing and where I was and what happened. Even now, there's nothing like the tangible things I bring home to satisfy that itch for proof I can touch.

I no longer think of myself as a garbage picker but rather the curator of a very curious museum whose only theme when it comes to displays is *whatever the hell I want it to be.* I still like fossils. I still collect shed antlers and just this past fall scored not only the biggest doe skull I've ever found, but also that of a wonderful ten-point buck which led me to place a new stand in an old, overlooked patch of woods. They're there on the hearth next to the bear skull from long, long ago. Sometimes in the summer when it's too warm to spend time in the mosquito-infested woods, or in the heart of winter when it's too cold even for this hardy outdoorsman, I pick them up and dust them off and remember the day I found them. Like the infinitely more impressive deer heads and bear mounts, they're a simple bridge to a moment spent in the outdoors. Since my moratorium on getting rid of any more was put in place, the collection has grown only modestly—but I'm always looking.

The museum is always open for business.

8

THE GHOSTS OF MAINE

THE BEAR was not mine. A bear can't be yours, no matter who you are and no matter how well you shot. You can't own them in a way that a pheasant or a grouse or a rabbit can be yours. You go to the places they live—strange places—and kill them. There is none of you in that place, but if you have been honest and hunted well, there may always be a part of that place in you. There's a certain sense of accomplishment in that, but it still doesn't make the bear yours. And this bear wasn't even *partially* mine. He belonged to the hunter next to me, as much as he could belong to anyone.

The night had an eerie sadness about it. The north woods roared by the open bed of the pickup and the four men in the back were mostly silent. It had been a long week and we had all hunted hard, but the bears were in the berries this year and were not coming to the baits. For me this evening's sunset darkened the last night of my second unsuccessful bear hunt over the course of three years. It wouldn't have been so aggravating for me except that I'd killed one my first time out and had been led to believe it could be quite easy, this business of bear hunting. In the bouncing bed of the pickup, with the moon shining brightly overhead, I thought maybe I was never meant to shoot another bear.

Thoughts like that make sense at times like these.

Hunters who come home empty-handed from a hunting trip are sad. Don't let them tell you otherwise. Of course they enjoyed the smell of the woods and they felt they were a part of nature—all of that—but they also descended into the alien world of wilderness on a mission, and at the end of a week such as this, there is a sense of failure. It's a very real element to big-game hunting. If everyone won, there wouldn't be much challenge in it.

When the pickup truck came late to pick me up, I knew someone had finally shot a bear. Having been party to some bear tracking in the past, I prayed that whoever shot it had killed cleanly. Bear tracking by the glow of a flashlight, while exciting, is perhaps too exciting. But when I climbed into the back of the truck, everyone else was there and the truck was lacking the distinctive smell of bear, though one of the men wore a large grin. His teeth shone white in the moonlight. The other three faces were as long as I imagined mine to be. Through the dirty window of the pickup truck, I tried to see the guide to see his expression. It was too dark to tell but, after the failures of this week, I'm sure his face matched most of the rest of ours in length.

Nothing is close in northern Maine and it was another twenty-five minutes of bouncing and eating dust before we arrived at the hunter's stand. He had been strangely silent for most of the ride, though he did manage to tell us he had put a clean kill on the bear. For that I was thankful.

Following the bobbing beams of the guide's lantern and everyone's flashlights down through the thick woods, with branches and ferns grabbing and pulling at us in the dark, we arrived at the dead bear.

Dead bears look nothing like live bears, other than in color. While a dead deer looks generally like a live deer lying on the ground and a dead pheasant looks remarkably like a live pheasant, a dead bear looks as if all its bones have been removed and the consistency of its body is like an extra large bean bag chair. With its air let out, a bear is simply a large, hairy, black blob that shifts like an under-filled water mattress when you try to move it. I could see the scuffmarks on the ground where the hunter and the guide had tried to drag it, but had been unsuccessful.

It was a big bear.

We all admired it there in the dark, briefly though because the night was growing long and we were all anxious to be done with the week. The hunter told of the steady parade of bears to the bait this afternoon. He'd seen no fewer than eight bears, mostly sows and cubs. The two males had come in shortly before dark, the second—this one—being far larger than the first. In the yellow glow of the flashlights, the other hunters and I went through another metamorphosis. Our faces grew even longer, if that was possible, as we each silently weighed the unfairness of this man seeing so many bears while we had all entertained nothing more than red squirrels and spruce grouse at our stands.

We clapped him on the back and shook his hand anyway. That's what you do.

Moving the bear, even with everyone taking a double hand-hold on the furry, shifting mass, was difficult. We ascended the slope to the logging road in halts and starts and the light never fell where your foot had to be planted next. Before we were done, everyone had slipped or fallen or turned an ankle. Finally at the truck, we were hot and bloody and smelled of bear fat.

The weight of the bear made the old truck sag on its springs even before we all piled in.

Only one man was smiling. (It wasn't me.)

In the truck, the hunter and I sat with our backs to the glass. He, with his legs stretched over the back of the bear that took up most of the bed, and me with its still-warm head resting on my thighs. It seemed almost sad to be taking him away from here, but I knew I would feel nothing but happiness if it had been my bear, as much as a bear can be yours.

The hunter held himself well. I dislike big-game hunters who brag too much, and I feel an even deeper distrust for the smug men who shrug their shoulders after success and say little, as if it was a foregone conclusion that they would kill a good animal. This man was excited and though he didn't talk too much out of respect for the unhappy hunters around him, he eagerly told me the details of his day in hushed, excited tones. I must have that kind of face. I'd long ago decided that it's okay to have that kind of face. The dark woods rushed past us. An occasional branch slapped at the fenders of the truck with a jumpy clank. The truck slowed too quickly once, and the men nearer the tail-gate held tightly and cursed lightly. When we finally ground to a stop, we all stood to watch the moose, a young cow, hurriedly trot through the glow of the headlights. Steam blasted from her nostrils against the night's chill.

While the man talked, now barely able to contain his excite-ment, I stroked the bear's long fur absently, much as I do with my bird dog when he comes sneaking under the table to beg scraps. The conversation was lost against the moonlight and the dust and the smell of the bear's great head resting on my lap.

For a moment—only one—he was mine. As much as a bear can be yours.

9

EARLY ON

PRIOR TO autumn there is a building excitement that crescendos with the first hunt of the year. For me that is either squirrels or geese. Early on in the season once that baptismal hunt is over, a calmness settles over me as I settle into the rhythm of the woods, once again welcomed to the place that I feel most at home. Later on, the excitement will again escalate. Before bear season, there's much anticipation. The days leading up to pheasant season reveal much fun and preparation, and throwing the dummy for Max to make sure he still knows how to retrieve. Later there are the bow hunts for deer and then the gun season that is the pinnacle of the hunting year.

But for now, early on, there are squirrel hunts, a handful of goose hunts in the Big Swamp, and just some general scouting. *Early on* has a charm all its own.

I hadn't hunted the area since Maggie was a puppy, and she's almost ten years gone, now. I considered bringing Max, but opted instead for my squirrel rifle, my GPS, and my camera. I wanted to cover some ground where I wanted to cover some ground. With Max, he leads the way and many of the directional decisions would have been out of my hands. My first vacation day of the year, I was excited to explore the pheasant fields and the deer woods of this small public hunting area about which I'd recently heard good things. A solo trip seemed just the ticket on a cool September morning. A solo trip always seems like a good idea.

Only a half mile onto the state land, I slammed on the brakes when a large rooster pheasant strutted across the dirt road, his head bobbing and narrowly averting death at the hands of some all-terrain tires. His timing couldn't be worse in this desolate area. I'm sure I was the only car to come along for hours, yet he decided to cross from one bean field to the next at that very moment. I not only believe in omens, but I encourage them. Certainly, it must be a sign that the place is loaded with pheasants. Right? Or it's just a sign that this is a place I should hunt. Or, it's just a pheasant, but what fun is that?

With no time to pull my better camera out of the pack in the back of the truck, I grabbed my smartphone off the dash. I snapped a couple of quick photos of the bird, but he didn't seem to mind as he pecked at some beans that, frankly, looked just the same as the beans on the other side of the road. He seemed to understand the difference. Why did the pheasant cross the road? I'm not quite sure, but I guess he had his reasons, funny or not.

I thought I recognized a few fields and thickets, but I wasn't sure. In the twenty years that had passed on the autumn breeze since last I set foot there, much had changed. It always does. The place was as new to me as if I'd never been there, and that's acceptable to me. If it was all familiar, it wouldn't be half as exciting. Parking just past the expansive bean fields, I hiked up two of the drainage ditches that fed a larger creek. The tiny, brush-choked draws were thick with deer sign. One of the ditches is bisected by a deer trail that comes down from the ridge high above the bean fields. I follow the trail for a half mile, paying close attention to the heavy deer tracks—tracks of all sizes—stamped into the soft ground. Mentally marking two or three places on the trail with an eye toward deer season, I then physically marked one more on the GPS when I jumped a small fork-horned buck bedded in the goldenrod and thistle. *Deer country.* Rather than backtrack my own footprints, which at the time seemed pointless, I followed up some lesser deer trails, tributaries of the main run. There were old buck rubs, a couple of brand new scrapes and, twice, deer jumped up in the long grass ahead of me as if they were rabbits flushing from a thornapple thicket with dogs hot on their heels. The place was ripe with deer.

Once back at my truck, I drove a short distance until I crossed a small creek in a deceptively deep ravine. There was an old marking from a horse trail, long since overgrown. I decided to explore. The freedom of September courses through my blood and there's nothing I'd *rather* do than explore an old horse trail above a ravine deep in the heart of deer country. What else would I do? Go home and watch TV?

Stepping off the rough dirt road, I quickly surveyed my parking job. I hoped that anyone else who happened to come along could squeeze past me, not wishing to worry about it once deep in the woods on what I hoped would be a long, productive hike. Fairly certain I was far enough off the road, I headed into the green oak woods of September.

A city-dwelling coworker of mine once gave me advice about my first visit to New York City. Among the other survival tips he gave me was to not look up, keep my eyes forward, and, above all, don't act like a tourist. Had that ravine been deep in Brooklyn instead of the peacefully mountainous surroundings of Wyoming County, New York, I'm sure I would have been mugged. Above me, ancient oak trees blotted out the sky. Stands of beech with gray trunks like impossibly lanky legs stretched upward, competing only with the oaks for sunlight. How old must these trees be? How many generations of hunters had walked through here on their own quest for solitude? How many more generations would even care? My head was on a swivel and my neck ached from craning skyward.

I wasn't mugged, despite my lack of situational awareness.

Deeper and deeper into the hardwoods, leaves crunched below me, miles passed, and I realized that the ravine was plunging farther and farther below me. The quiet music of the creek, loud at the outset of my hike, was now a muted tinkling hundreds of feet below. When I realized how far down it was, I paid more attention to my footing and less to the treetops. The thick carpet of large oak leaves—mostly large, smooth white oaks looking like a million small human hands reaching up from the forest floor—was littered with acorns. New green acorns, old brown acorns, and many clumps of branches with leaves and acorns still attached and still green with the season's fresh growth covered the ground. I knew the place must be thick with squirrels.

Checking my GPS a few times, surprised at how far I'd wandered from the truck, I hadn't yet found a place so loaded with sign that it warranted deer hunting in the fall. A few hundred yards farther, I came across a small rivulet cutting through the leaves, bare rock exposed from thousands of years of erosion. Deer droppings and acorns littered the north side of the brook as I headed deeper into the woods and away from the ravine. Where the brook split a few hundred yards above, there stood a small stand of beech and three wild apple trees in a small, open grove. A crossroads of four different deer trails met on the far side of the brook.

This was the place.

Well removed from the road, there was abundant food and water, and enough deer sign that a traffic light wouldn't have been unwarranted at the crossing. I immediately sat down at the base of a large oak, slinging my pack and rifle off my shoulder with a great deal of relief. Marking the coordinates on my GPS, I fished through the pack for a water bottle. Four miles into the woods in uncharted territory, I'd finally found a spot to deer hunt this fall and decided that I had earned a break.

The break didn't last long, maybe thirty seconds. A flash above me in the beech canopy gave me a start. Grabbing my rifle, my thoughts returned from some future deer hunt and I focused on the hunt at hand. I found the gray in the scope but—just as on my first hunt out on the peninsula back home—the animal disappeared as I began pulling the trigger. Before I could lower the rifle, a fight erupted inside the tree above me as the previous occupant of the hole apparently was in no mood for company. The black squirrel popped out of the hole, still chattering away and indignant at his eviction. Racing down the tree, he stopped just opposite me. I've seen a few and missed one a few years ago, but black-phase gray squirrels have always enticed me. There aren't many of them in my hunting areas. I was happier retrieving him from the base of the tree than you probably should be about killing a squirrel.

Snapping a few photos on my smartphone, I sent them to my small circle of hunters. There's John, now retired in Florida who won't be back to New York until deer season. Porter is at college, and there's Steve who was probably working today. I hit send and the congratulatory replies came back instantly. John and I used to work together, and taunt each other with fish and game photos sent to the person who happened to be working that day. Now that he's retired, he does more sending than receiving. Since early in the days of camera phones, I earned every moment of that abuse. This would just be the beginning of our autumn communications. We seldom get the chance to hunt together anymore and faithfully keep each other updated with our successes and, often, our failures. In the next couple of months, there would be coyote photos and several deer photos from Porter and John. Steve would send a photo of my nephew Eric and his first doe. I'd send photos of the first woodcock and Max's pheasant successes. I sometimes regret taking my phone into the woods and fields because it's too easy for work to pester me, but I do like keeping in touch and, in this case, doing a little bragging. There's something to be said for twenty-first-century technology and its outdoor applications.

Satisfied from my morning success with the black squirrel, and adding another small pin on my GPS map (full of hunting locations whose satellite images I would look up later), I followed the brook back to the steep ravine. Overcoming my fear of heights long enough to peer over the edge, the view was dizzying, not at all hinted at by the shallow saddle back where the brook crossed the road. I perched on a stump for a bit, and was not surprised when another gray squirrel appeared on the trunk of a large oak fifty yards from me. The rifle cracked and I added the squirrel to the pack, after sending a few more photos, of course . . .

Nearing the road, another black squirrel crossed my path and scurried up an old hemlock. Despite waiting him out, he never reappeared, not in the time I was willing to invest waiting, anyway. Sweaty and tired from the hiking, I stood once again above the brook, now only a few dozen feet below me in the saddle, and pondered. *Oh, what the hell.* The walk down into the brook was easier than I thought despite the protests of my aching bones. I hunted for fossils in the exposed shale for another half hour, keeping my pack and rifle nearby, feeling like that young boy picking up owl pellets and turkey feathers back home all those years ago.

It's a good thing to feel like that.

Farther on up the road, I pulled off the soft shoulder in a place that had looked good on Google Earth. On Actual Earth, it didn't look so good, with just a smattering of hardwoods in a sea of hemlock. Driving on, I kicked up dust for another mile. I spotted a beaver pond and then another small ravine cutting the road on both sides. Beech woods rose on one side of the road and oaks dropped off on the other. Hiking down into the oak side, only because downhill sounded good (with a bit of denial about the hike back up and out, of course), I found several deer trails crossing from some goldenrod fields above, and down into the beeches. Far below, several tight funnels of underbrush lined the dry creek bed. From above, this was the perfect vantage point for a deer hunt. Finding a suitable rock (one, as I'd discover later in the season, I was not the first to find), I marked it on my GPS. The sprawling view of two divergent creek beds and several narrow fingers of beech and oak was a panorama of classic deer country, while the closer of the two creek beds below marked *my* kind of deer country. It was brushy, dense, and barely penetrable. I scanned the low country with my scope, ostensibly looking for squirrels but instead finding several of last year's buck rubs. Sometimes it's not all about scenic beauty. Sometimes it's just about feeling that *feeling,* and I felt it. Walking out, I kept an eye out for squirrels, but barely. My bones ached from the day's activity but my mind was already in November.

On the way out, not far from where the pheasant had crossed the road, I jammed on the brakes as a doe and two fawns leapt the ditch in graceful bounds to land out in the road. The last fawn nearly earned a headlight imprint in his ass, but it was worth knocking everything off the backseat to avoid hitting it. I watched them go for a few moments, not surprised when they slowed to a walk only fifty yards into the expansive bean field and began feeding in plain sight. Deer season couldn't come soon enough, and in those few short minutes at the intersection of the two dry creek beds, I already had decided where I'd spend opening day. It's a good feeling to know something like that. I didn't hunt fossils on the way out this time. Lost in thought, for a few moments I was already into the future, wishing the days away between now and November. Wishing the days away is a sin and one that I accept as my worst personality flaw. I own that. That anticipation, however, is all part of the magic.

Leaving the hunting area for the day, I wouldn't return until pheasant season. I savored sprawling views of the rounded hillsides and steep ravines, the oak ridges and the crop fields. Not for the first time, I tried to picture the places Maggie and I had hunted when we came here hunting grouse and wood-cock twenty years ago. Unlike my hunting grounds back home, which are as familiar as my own backyard, nothing looked familiar. Everything seemed new. Twenty years spans at least two dog lives. The fields had probably become brush, and the saplings had become trees, while still other places where we may have set foot were now planted in corn or beans or soy. Nothing was the same. How could it be? Nature had moved on, as always, to the next season.

Maybe I had, too.

10

THE GHOST OF HANGING BOG

ON MY way home from the scouting and squirreling trip, I took a twenty-mile detour to Hanging Bog, another hunting area in my corner of the state. Less polished and rounded than the foothills I just left, the three-thousand-acre tract is dense, steep, and rocky. Quite happy with my take of two squirrels, especially the prized black squirrel, I would have been content to head home for the day. However, I'd so enjoyed the morning's hunt and exploration that I decided to drop in for a quick hunt not far from the road, as a reward to my aching feet.

On the way in, I couldn't help smiling as I passed a field of cut sweet corn stretching from the dirt road almost impossibly far to the south where it terminated in a dense pine stand. I felt pity for whoever had to pick that cornfield.

The field was worth surveying, only because on an early hunt a few years ago, my brother-in-law and I had driven on this same dirt road up into the mountains on a foggy morning when he calmly said, "Look—someone's cow is out." Indeed, through the fog it looked like a cow for about ten seconds. It was, in fact, the biggest black bear I've ever seen in my life. It didn't look like a *small* cow. It looked like a *cow.* Snatching my camera from the backseat, I opened my door and raced around the back of the truck. The bear, of course, was having nothing of it and sprinted three hundred yards in an incredibly short amount of time. I got some pictures, just a black blur in the fog. One of the photos even looks bearlike. Sort of.

That had been a squirrel-hunting day, but I spent the rest of the morning in the woods thinking only of bear hunting. I also spent a good deal of my time in a nearby creek bottom checking over my shoulder more frequently than I ever had on a squirrel hunt. It was a *big bear.* I couldn't afford a bear hunt that year, but by the end of the week I had one booked and had made travel plans to Maine. Sometimes nature just sends you a message.

Sometimes I wish it would send cash.

Sitting in a small finger of hemlocks high above the same creek bottom where the big bear had disappeared a few years ago, I was pleased with the day, lost in old memories while planning new ones. Maybe a bear hunt? No . . . not this year. Too expensive. *Must . . . resist . . .*

Later in the day, with still a few hours of my vacation time to burn, I headed again to the woods, this time near home. Joy had several times spotted deer feeding in a small bean field at the edge of a small wood lot where I used to have permission to hunt. I didn't think much of it. Though she'd been seeing them there frequently as deer season approached, I hadn't hunted there in years. A chance encounter in a local restaurant, however, put me back in touch with the landowner. Don Robinson, the farmer who owns that little peace of heaven, was my first real boss when I was a teenager. I learned more in those summers working on the farm than I did in high school and college combined. I did everything from picking sweet corn at dawn so it didn't get sunburned, to finally graduating to driving the tractor during planting season, and eventually loading the market truck at night with Don and his dad, Chester, the patriarch of the farm. I can't tell you all the lessons I learned there, but I can tell you that I learned how to *work*. And—Don made sure of this—I also learned that it wasn't a good work day if you didn't have some fun along the way. After bumping into Don in the restaurant thirty years later, I decided to call and ask permission to hunt. He said he never forgot a good worker (and offered me a job picking tomatoes!) and that I could hunt anytime I wanted. I asked him how the farm business was and was delighted in his reply: "We have a lot of fun."

Though I had my twenty-two again slung on my shoulder, I didn't want to shoot the woods up with deer season fast approaching. However, if a black squirrel or some other highly desirable and exotic game animal happened to cross my path, it's always good to be prepared. Just a few feet into the woods, I knew I wouldn't be shooting anything, exotic or not. The deer trails crisscrossed everywhere in the old hardwoods, occasionally following old tractor paths, and sometimes ducking into dense undergrowth. Old rubs were everywhere. I wasted no time backtracking the trails out to the field where Joy had spotted the deer. Oh boy. There were tracks everywhere. Fawn tracks, buck tracks, large tracks, small tracks. One track, two track, red track, blue track. The field had a wedge from the edge of the woods where the beans had been picked clean from each and every plant. This was a gold mine. Back inside the woods, I followed an old rub line and came across the first true ghost of autumn. A ten-point buck, his skeleton complete and intact, lay on the deer trail along the rub line, perfectly undisturbed. He'd been traveling west into the woods, and his nose was centered on the trail. I snatched up the tremendous skull and the pair of bleached white scapulas (I don't know why—I think I've already mentioned that I'm a *curator* at a very exclusive museum, didn't I?) and retreated back to deposit them at an obvious spot in the trail. If that buck wasn't a sign, nothing ever was. Paying attention to the signs is a big part of what a successful hunting season is all about.

My squirrel hunt ended, morphing into a speed-scouting trip as I quickly surveyed the rest of the small wood lot. Unlike the place farther to the south, not much had changed here in the last fifteen years. I knew right where I wanted to put a stand. Racing quickly home, I picked up a ladder stand and returned to Robinson's woods. Dragging the clanking metal beast into the small woods, I leaned it against my selected oak tree and strapped it as high up as I could before climbing. I've done this a long time and I *know* that putting a ladder stand up is a two-person job. I made it almost to the top when the ladder leaned away from the tree and stood straight upright for a moment as I held on helplessly waiting to either fall or slam back into the tree.

I didn't fall, but did climb down quickly and call Joy for help. When she arrived, I scrambled back up with a little less confidence and a fair amount of shakiness. Joy did her best to steady the ladder as I ascended what suddenly seemed like a needlessly tall stand with a series of colorful words, many of which I undoubtedly learned in the fields up on the ridge while picking tomatoes many decades ago. Joy was as relieved as I when the ladder was finally secured to the tree.

We have a lot of fun.

11

THE CIRCLE

I AM not antisocial. I am not *extremely* antisocial, anyway.

One of the things inherent in being a person who is passionate about something as time-consuming as hunting is how it can undermine your social life. Being an outdoorsman, with scouting and hunting preparations to be attended to year-round, you might assume that I shouldn't really be worrying about a full-fledged social life anyway. It's not something I've ever desired. When one hunting season or another doesn't find me slogging around in the fields and woods, that's only because it's fishing season. Or, as now, by the fire: writing season. The keys click away, and memories flow freely from the autumn in my mind to the blank computer screen in front of me. The hours and days pass, the months pass, and the pages fill. And the phone, when it rings, is not usually for me.

Like hunting, writing is often a lonely endeavor. It has to be. It's too easy to break those tenuous threads that connect *then* to *now*, that allow the memories to live on the page. For me, being alone isn't the same thing as being lonely. Far from it.

I've learned to embrace aloneness, and that is in no way the same thing as accepting loneliness. While I long for aloneness especially when life is getting thick and bogged down, I have thus far managed to elude loneliness.

It used to bother me when my only regular social interactions occurred during the fleeting, precious months of fall. The other months are spent writing, working around the house, fishing, playing guitar in a band, and, of course, working at my real job. They are full months, but many of them pass without once hearing from my "hunting buddies." After years of insecurity, I've developed a different view of friendship. The last few years it has dawned on me that my hunting friends *are* my friends. To some people, many of whom have said so, it might seem odd that good friendships could survive over the months-long void of spring and summer. But they do.

I'm not saying that I only talk to my friends in September, October, and November. That would be an exaggeration and I want to save my exaggerating for later pages. There are, however, some friends at the far edge of my circle of hunting friends whom I *only* talk to during hunting season. Would *you* call people like that friends? I don't know if you might, but I do. There is a group of people with whom I've shared more in a few days together than I would in a month with someone else. I think it's a phenomenon uniquely understood by hunters. So much has been written on camaraderie that the word has lost its edge, like a knife that's cleaned one too many birds since its last sharpening. There's more to it than handshakes and backslaps. It's not as simple as bloody hands and greasy diners, dirty jokes and clouds of steam from gales of laughter in the cold air. There's far more at stake than tired dogs and pants full of burrs. There will be fond memories shared with people I care about, and mourning for those we've lost. Like the outdoors we love, there will be sunlight and there will be shadows. Hunting season is such a special part of the year, such a large part of my life, that it is fitting that the majority of my friends are my hunting friends. It took me a while to realize and accept that, but as the years march on, it makes more sense.

The season is almost here and it will just as soon be over. The frantic pace that will be maintained for the next fifty or so days will wind down to a quiet and not altogether unpleasant case of burnout. Just as sure as hunting season has arrived, the afterglow of exhaustion will take its place in late December. The phone that has rung off the hook after sunset nearly every night will again be silent. Unlike the rest of the year, the calls are almost *always* for me as my friends come in from their stands, full of stories, full of excitement, and quite often full of shit. And then there will be no more calls. And that's okay.

It's a funny thing, this concept of friendship. Just like the places where we spend our time in pursuit of whatever it is we happen to be pursuing this time, my relationships with those around me are always in motion, constantly changing. Sometimes they evolve and improve and sometimes they wither and die, but they're never the same. Like nature, friendship is never in balance. It ebbs and flows. Times of plenty give way to times of want. Like any other natural function, friendship is always seeking that middle ground that it is doomed never to find. But like hunting, the true meaning of friendship is not always in the finding, but in the seeking.

As I did with the black squirrel, I eagerly send John, Porter, and Steve the photos of the recovered ten-point skull. My phone dings almost instantly with the first reply.

It's the twenty-first century and hunting season has just begun.

12

THE WOODS NEAR NOBLEBORO BRIDGE

THERE ARE many places that live in my daydreams. In my mind, they're much more vivid and alive than a mark on a map or a coordinate on my GPS or a satellite photo from Google Earth. I could take you to the quiet Catskill mountaintop brook where I shot my first buck and my fourth, and my seventh, eighth, and ninth, a coyote, a five-gallon pail full of squirrels, and several more bucks after that. It's quite a hike, but I've no doubt you'd like the place. I could drive you to the place in Maine where I shot that first big bear. Strike that, I could drive you to the place (dodging logging trucks and cow moose along the way) where we'd launch the boat and carefully thread our way upriver through the boulders. We'd beach the beaten jon boat at a tiny sandy landing where there's just enough room to wedge it in between the treacherous boulders. From there, a short hike up to a notch in two granite outcroppings where the bear dropped. I could even show you where the gut pile was. I could take you to the place in Michigan's Upper Peninsula where I shared bourbon and shot woodcock with another writer, Marty

Kovarik, whom I'd only ever met in a writer's group on the Internet. I was not surprised when we hit it off and even less surprised when we had a spectacular weekend of dog talk and bird shooting and storytelling. I could drive you right to the spot where his Brittany flushed the first woodcock of the week. It's just past the railroad tracks, right before the pond.

All these places live in my mind. Though I love adventure and enjoy travel and would like to see the *rest* of the world, most of my bucket list consists simply of returning to places that have meant the world to me. I've already seen heaven and I want to go back.

Nobleboro Bridge is one of those places.

There's a bridge that crosses the West Canada Creek near Nobleboro, in the shadow of Fort Noble Mountain. I just call it Nobleboro Bridge, though I'm sure the locals, what few there are, probably call it something else. Above the small dam the brook trout are uneducated, unwary, and unbelievably tasty. I've canoed the upper reaches of the creek and eaten shore lunches of brookies and the occasional large pike, present because they also find the supply of brook trout irresistible.

Several years in a row, all those years ago, I took Maggie for a few overnight trips and we killed woodcock and tried to kill grouse, on the banks of the creek and up into the beech slashings. We never had much luck but there were enough birds to keep us coming back. Used to the overgrown farmlands back home, Maggie seemed equally at home in the big woods. She wasn't nearly as distracted by the breathtaking scenery as I. Sometimes I think it would be wonderful to be a dog, but at times like that I felt bad that her dog personality could never enjoy the sprawling views of the summit of Fort Noble Mountain, so engrossed was she in hunting. Maybe she did and she was just more focused than I. Of that I have little doubt. On one of those high-mountain excursions, the weather turned too warm for man and beast, so we wrapped up our weekend hunt early, packing the tent hastily into the truck and pondering the level in my gas tank compared to the calculated gas mileage of the five-hour drive. Driving more slowly than one who was about to embark down a long road home, I navigated the truck slowly up the dirt road that would eventually become another dirt road, and finally a main road. I didn't want to go, but it was too damned hot and there were miles to go before I slept.

With peripheral vision homed in the deer woods for long enough to matter, I spotted motion out the passenger-side window. Paralleling my truck on the remote dirt road was an eight-point whitetail buck with velvet antlers of significant proportions. I hit the brakes hard enough to nearly send Maggie into the dashboard. My truck was an unexpected intrusion into the big deer's mountain life and unlike the deer back home, he simply stopped to see what we were. Had we been home in more developed Niagara County, the buck would have been making lodging arrangements in the next county over if not the next state. Not this one, though. He just paused to observe.

So did I.

Rolling down the window, I snatched the Nikon from the backseat. The resulting pictures were no clearer than if they'd been lifted from the Patterson–Gimlin film. Inconclusive though they might be, I still have the photos. They don't matter. If I took them today I'd delete them as being subpar examples of my photography skills. The day didn't matter, but, then again, it did. I haven't deleted those photos and with good reason. In retrospect, I realize that every day afield has been a lesson and a brick of memory added to the wall that we all look back on and call life. It was no mistake that the following November I returned to the rock ridge above West Canada Creek and for the first time in my life, I deer hunted that very spot just west of the pond and just north of the river.

I never killed a deer at Nobleboro. I've seen *many* deer but never had a good shot, or never had a doe tag when I spotted an antlerless deer. The year I saw a good buck, I was only hunting does, having filled my tag back home. I saw bears, but never shot a bear here. Their claw marks marked the ancient beeches, handholds to the treetops that were scarred from decades of climbing for the sweet mast above.

The place is not my nemesis, just another place that drew me back, time and time again. Its gifts were not venison or trophies or memories of exciting hunts. The gifts were more extrinsic, exotic. Nobleboro was *fun*. Nobleboro *is* fun.

Raised in the flat farmland of western New York, I'd cut my outdoor teeth in the mountains of the Adirondacks. When I was barely old enough to walk, my parents took me up Goodnow Mountain—not very far from Nobleboro. When I was a child on vacation with my parents, and later, a teenager, I caught toothy, smiling northern pike in the cold, deep reaches of Loon Lake. At night, we fished for bullhead with my grandfather (one of my best memories of him) in the warm shallows of that same lake, and I learned that a dinner you caught or killed yourself tasted far better than that which some indifferent middleman might have to offer. Still just a kid in my twenties, I brought my own daughters to Loon Lake, to these mountains, and tried—though I was likely no damned good at it at the time—to show them what it meant to be in the wilderness. To learn from it. To grow because of it. To be a part of nature, rather than to read about it in a book or watch it on the Discovery Channel. I fished there. I hunted there. I never had a bad day there, despite snow and rain and thunder and sleet, or heat and humidity, mosquitoes and ticks. The woods near Nobleboro Bridge, lying high above the West Canada Creek, represent all that is good and wild in my life. I shared it with just a handful of people, most of them very close friends and family. I'd like to think it still lives in their hearts as well.

Twenty years later it is still a magical place. Maybe more so. There aren't many places in my notes and photos with a legendary status, but Nobleboro Bridge and the surrounding mountainsides are as enchanted as any place I've ever known. I can't cross that bridge to this day without slowing to remember brook trout and pike and woodcock and bears and deer.

I wish everyone had such a place.

My nephew Porter is an outstanding outdoorsman. He has the right combination of obsessive work ethic, luck, and love of the outdoors. In his short hunting career, he's killed several bucks and he just sent me the photos of a tremendous coyote. Everything he has killed, he has earned. His respect for the outdoors and outdoor ethics puts him at the top of the list of the favorite hunters in my small circle. He and I haven't spent a lot of time hunting together. Just a few small game hunts and a couple of deer hunts. Nonetheless, he enjoys most-favored-hunter status with me. On top of everything else, his enthusiasm for all things wild and adventurous reminds me of someone near and dear to my heart. It's only natural that I introduced him to the woods around Nobleboro Bridge. If anyone could appreciate Nobleboro, it's Porter.

The five-hour drive from home involved a mild case of windshield wiper–induced hypnosis followed by the steady steep climb into the Adirondack Mountain range where the rain was replaced by freezing rain. The freezing rain was pushed aside by sleet, and finally, just a dozen miles from the bridge, wet snowflakes. Where I'm from, the white stuff is a fact of life, but I still get excited by the first snowflakes of the year. Each of those first Adirondack flakes, nonetheless, was October's white flag of surrender to winter.

Just a mile from the bridge, struggling to see through the constantly fogging windshield and the large wet flakes, I locked up the brakes just in time as a big whitetail doe blew off the steep bank to my right and into my path. The pedal vibrated sickly under my foot as the truck slowed just enough on the icy road to not hit her. Once my heart stopped pounding, and I was sure she was safely to the other side, I decided to take the sighting as another good omen. I didn't need to make an appointment at a body shop, and she would live to help populate one of my favorite hunting areas. *Win-win.* No sense being negative about it. I drove the remaining mile a bit more slowly.

Porter was there when I arrived, his running lights the only beacon in the stormy mountain pre-dawn. We parked at the small scenic overlook and I quickly explained where we'd be driving from there. It was miserable, wet and cold, but the excitement was palpable as we changed out of our travel clothes and into our hunting gear before heading up the dark dirt road. The storm had knocked down a few trees, and we were able to thread our way around them and continue up, West Canada Creek falling off far below us in the gathering gloomy daylight. When I spotted the small pond at the base of a steep rise, I pulled over. It had been a while since my last hunt in this vast wilderness, but I knew it was close enough.

I hurriedly explained to Porter that I was simply going to climb the high ridge above the creek and find a good vantage point, simple as that. I told him that the rocks are treacherous on a good day, and advised him to be careful since this day was anything but good. I suggested a trajectory for Porter and told him that if he got lost, all he had to do was head downhill and listen for the river below because it would always guide him back to the dirt road. Our hushed wishes of *good luck* were the first sounds of deer season.

Sunrise happened beneath the dense mountain clouds, but it happened. Gray dawn turned into brighter gray daylight. The climb was steeper than I remembered. Trying to pace myself,

I paused often while ascending the beech ridge. Higher on the ridge, the rain was more firmly committed to turning to snow. Straining to see Porter to the east, I assumed he was probably already at the top. There was a fifteen-foot-high boulder with two-foot stepping stones on its uphill side, a natural stairway. I didn't tell Porter but that's where I directed him, hoping he'd find my favorite spot in all of the Adirondacks. A natural elevated stand, it gave not only a sprawling view of the deer trails and bear caves below, but also a commanding view of the river and of Fort Noble Mountain. Had I been hunting alone, I would have gone there myself, but I wanted Porter to find it. I wanted it to be his.

Almost at the top, I cleared out a patch of leaves at the base of an old ash and rested for a few moments, taking a drink of water and ridding my shoulder of the muzzleloader and heavy pack for a bit. Below me the river churned, muted thunder enhanced by the previous night's rain. Above me, barely visible through the snow, rose the gray shadow of Fort Noble Mountain. Its rounded peak more reminiscent of a Catskill hill than an Adirondack mountain, the familiar landmark was comforting in the rugged woods. I hoped that Porter was in place and seeing the same sight and thinking the same things in his own way. I glanced at my phone, just to check the time, but I noticed that there was no cell signal. *There shouldn't be*, I thought, not at all remorseful that no one at work could contact me if any problems arose. I hoped, not just for my own benefit, but for the next generation of outdoor lovers, that the beech ridge above West Canada Creek never saw more than one bar of cell signal. That is as it should be. At that moment, finally immersed in the wilderness that I so often crave, I hunkered down into my hunting parka and listened. No cars. No planes. What I heard was all that I need to hear: the rushing of a river full of trout, the brittle whisper of snow tapping against the beech leaves that have stubbornly hung on against the coming winter, and the sound of perfect solitude. It was the uninterrupted sound of nature as it now exists in so few places. A pileated woodpecker tapped somewhere down near the river, its staccato pounding impossibly loud in the quiet mountains. Back home, I probably would have missed it altogether against the din. I closed my eyes for a moment. Breathing in the cold, fresh air, I gave thanks.

With no break in the wet snow, I pulled myself up and slogged steeply upward, my footfalls muted by the wet leaves. A rock outcropping was my approximate destination, but I didn't mind if I ended up somewhere else. The entire upper ridge was a travel route for deer, and all I needed to do was plop myself down and hope the deer were moving. The deer here weren't plentiful, but they were consistent. Food, water, and cover down both sides of the ridge, steep enough to evade predators, offered them enough to keep them in the area in the harsh Adirondack cold.

Almost at the top of the ridge, as the air swirled with snow and motion, I was shocked when I spotted a deer leg in the beech slash to my left. I've hunted for a long time and know that being ready at a moment's notice is part of it, but I still fumbled. When I frantically grabbed for the rifle on my shoulder, the sling caught the backpack strap. My heavy pack slipped down one side of my body.

Idiot, I thought to myself as I dropped the heavy lump to the ground and flipped up my scope covers. The deer leg was still there. That I hadn't sent the deer packing with my clumsy gyrations was testament to how few hunters these deer have interacted with. Maybe she hadn't seen me at all. I don't know. Kneeling for a better angle, I felt the water coming in through my waterproof coveralls. I caught glimpses of lower legs, and every now and then a glimpse of her snout vacuuming up beechnuts. One longer look revealed it was a doe. I had a tag and would take her. She would be my first Nobleboro deer and a fine trophy after years of climbing this ridge. Only eighty yards from me the brush was so thick it might as well have been a thousand. The doe seemed completely unaware of me as I too was shielded by the dense saplings. Twice I took the safety off when it looked like a shoulder was going to emerge in a small hole in the brush. When I was younger, I'd taken worse shots through thicker brush and killed deer, but I wanted this one to be perfect.

It didn't happen.

Before I could squeeze the trigger with any degree of confidence that I wasn't going to shoot a tree (something that plagued me during a recent deer season), she disappeared over the rock ridge out of sight. Moving slowly to the edge, I peered out between two huge boulders with a sweeping view of the ridge below. As so often happens in deer hunting, it seemed as if the doe had simply disappeared. Hundreds of yards of open woods sprawled out before me and I could see almost down to the road. I took a seat and waited to catch a glimpse of motion on the hillside below me. Certain that she couldn't be far, I sat motionless for an hour before I began shivering from the wet and cold. She never did show, but when I stood to move, I spotted the trail she used to sneak along the ridge just below me. Perhaps she saw or heard me at the last moment. Maybe a cold swirl of mountaintop breeze had wafted my suspicious scent in her direction. *Near miss*, but I was no less thrilled to have my first close encounter of deer season.

Especially here.

I found the giant rock outcropping a half mile up the ridge and climbed up on a large wet boulder. After the slippery ascent, I decided that the last time I climbed up here I must have been much younger and much more careless. I am afraid of heights and had no desire to get too near the edge of the boulder, but the view was dizzying, amazing. It was breathtaking. The beech woods dotted with orange leaves stood out against the ground, now dusted white with snow. Below me, a small draw with an even smaller brook held imaginary brook trout. Punctuated with moss-covered boulders, it was guarded by giant wood ferns on its way down to the river below. Several beech trees towered above the saplings, wearing the scars of years of bear claws. Generation after generation of bears had used those handholds to reach the beechnuts and nap in the sunshine. For a few moments every black rock on the ridge turned into a bear as my binoculars got their best workout in years. Trying to disappear down into the collar of my coat, I settled onto my perch at my favorite place on Earth. Up here, everything seemed possible. Nothing seemed important but the moment. A light-snow fog blanketed the woods around me and at that instant, I tried to remember why it was so long since my last visit. *I should come here every day*, I decided. *This is what I need.*

When I was younger, time on the stand—even when the deer were plentiful—always seemed to pass slowly. It no longer does. There are few times remaining in my life, except the occasional family gathering, where time passes slowly. Time moves more quickly with each passing year. The morning high on the ridge above West Canada Creek was not exempt from that truth. Leaving myself barely enough time to get back to the road, I started downhill, following a brook (which turned out to be the wrong brook) back in the direction of our trucks. Emerging only a few hundred yards off course on the dirt shoulder, I wasn't entirely unpleased with the detour. Porter and I wolfed sandwiches, told a few stories, and enjoyed the break. After loaning Porter a dry pair of gloves, we quickly disappeared back up into our own personal tracts of the vast wilderness area. Despite the rain and snow I was eager to explore the ridge top again. The afternoon high above the river gave way to a chilly breeze and a decrease in the persistent precipitation.

The nature of the wild, rugged land and the distance we both had to drive—me back home, Porter back to college—saw us plan sensibly to meet back up at the truck around three. If one or both of us had a deer or, God help us, a bear to drag out of these slippery, rocky woods, it wouldn't be wise to hunt until dark. Half an hour before three, I slowly and reluctantly worked my way down. Descending the glossy white hillside, I paused here and there less to look for game and more to get fresh memories to take home. I hoped they'd tide me over until whenever I next set foot here, whether a month or five years from now. The roar of the river was loud and I knew the road was close. When the trucks came into view, shiny metal things in a sea of muted brown and tan and orange, an unequivocal sadness came over me. I wondered how long it *would* be before I hunted here again. Time certainly wouldn't slow down between now and then, so I made a pact with myself at least to return for an afternoon of brook trout fishing in the summer. Almost back at the trucks, I spotted orange through the woods to the east. Porter, too, was making his way back down.

Only, he wasn't.

It took a moment to focus, but my nephew—blessed with the good luck of a new hunter—was on one knee, just as I'd been early this morning. His gun was up, pointed toward the ridge. Was he just going to unload his muzzleloader into a stump before the trip home? He wouldn't do that, knowing I was still hunting and that he might spook deer. There was only one other answer. I crouched as well, suddenly knowing for certain that Porter was about to shoot *something.* Straining to see into the woods above him, I could barely make out his orange form, much less what he had in his sights. I saw the plume of smoke before I heard the thunderous roar from his muzzleloader. Branches broke above us. Porter, just turning in my direction and spotting me, held his hands and his rifle up in the air in a triumphant gesture. I could barely believe it. When he waved me over, I covered the distance more quickly than I thought possible.

Much more calm than I, Porter told me he'd just gotten back to the trucks when he spotted two deer coming down the hillside. He had paralleled them for a short distance, realizing they were does, and when the shot presented itself, just as I happened to be coming into view, he shot the big one. It went slightly uphill into a tangle of hemlocks and disappeared, but he was sure he'd made a good shoulder hit. We found the patch of kicked-up leaves. Gouts of blood painted the wet leaves. A few feet more and it had sprayed everywhere. Just a few yards farther we recovered the first deer I've ever seen killed in the woods near Nobleboro Bridge. Porter's calm demeanor was replaced by excitement.

Had no one pulled the trigger it would have been a successful trip. Sharing my favorite place with my favorite hunting partner and just breathing the air on that high, lonely ridge for a day would have been plenty to make it a wonderful, wet day in the mountains during deer season. For one of us to kill a deer here was far beyond my expectations. I did tell Porter to expect to see deer, so I was relieved to have come through in that regard.

I do enjoy being right.

After photos, Porter set about the dirty work of gutting the deer while I hiked back up the road with our packs and guns to get one of the trucks. At that moment, I couldn't have been more content. It's certainly not the first time I've felt contentment in the woods near Nobleboro Bridge.

When the deer was loaded we shook hands, talking only briefly as we slipped out of our soaked hunting gear and into dry clothes, preparing to head in separate directions. While Porter cleaned his hands in the brook near the road, I paused at the bridge, waiting for him. Three small blemishes of sunlight appeared through the gloom on Fort Noble Mountain. Grabbing my small camera from the dashboard, I snapped a photo of the mountain. Now hanging above my writing desk, it's a pretty good photo.

The memory in my heart from that day, however, is even sweeter.

13

THE GHOSTS IN THE DARKNESS

THE FIRST night of bow season near home brought me back to the reality of Niagara County and its precious few deer. With reports from Joy about the deer feeding in the bean fields and a new ladder stand in place to intercept them, I had hopes that were higher than the validity of those hopes. My hometown is a tough place to kill deer.

The afternoon passed as so many on a deer stand do. There were squirrels and birds and, unfortunately, a relentless wind as is so often the case there in the flatlands. I passed the time scanning the woods, counting the squirrels and putting the imaginary bead of my twenty-two rifle on them. Squirrel season was only a few days ago and as much as I love that early part of the hunting season, it was long gone. It had been *years* since I hunted here, and I was glad to be back in familiar territory that was both close to home and full of memories of years past. To the east stood an old oak against which I'd leaned another even more treacherous ladder stand years ago. Much like the woods near the bridge at Nobleboro, I'd never killed a deer there (yes, if you're wondering, there *are* places I've killed deer) but I saw one hell of a lot of them over the years. My fondest memories from this particular white oak stand in the small wood lot came when a thunderstorm rolled in. Just as I was preparing to climb down—youth be damned, I didn't want to be hit by lightning in a tall metal ladder stand—a line of deer appeared. Ten of them in all, the last was a fine buck with eight or more points. I watched them pass at fifty yards, helpless with my bow to do anything about it. A short series of grunts on my deer call did nothing to distract the big buck from the long line of real ladies. I didn't blame him.

I saw many deer over the years in those hardwoods, but never killed one. I killed squirrels, rabbits, and a pair of unlucky coons that were sunning themselves during the late squirrel season on a bitter cold day, but never a deer. It didn't stop me from trying for a while. Eventually, though, I did.

With sunset creeping in I'd hoped the wind would calm and the deer would begin moving. Though the deer may have started moving, the wind only gained in intensity as the sun set behind the wood lot on the opposite side of the road, illuminating the sky in vivid orange against the swaying limbs and trunks around me. It became apparent that there would be no magical reprieve from the strong wind close to dark, so I unbuckled my safety harness, feeling the tree sway as I climbed down. Unlike some of my other hunting places, the walk out to the truck was comically short. Such is the lot in life of the small wood lot hunter. I can see my truck from the stand if I hold my head just right. The road noise was constant. I thought briefly of the silence at Nobleboro. This place also had its charms, though; I did not feel cheated just because it was not a vast wilderness area. Nature was here too.

In the small clearing by the road, movement to my left caused me to stop in my tracks. Only a hundred yards from the road, I spotted the silhouettes of two deer near the edge of the woods. So common with deer around here, when the wind kicked up they'd picked an open area where they could more easily hear trouble coming their way. I ducked behind the cover of some tall phragmites staking out their survival along a tiny drainage ditch. The cover was sparse, but it was something, and there was still daylight to spare.

With just enough hope to keep things interesting, I crouched and moved slowly along the backside of the tall reeds, pausing where a natural opening presented itself in the area I thought the deer might be. They were. Both were feeding under the outstretched branches of a small red oak that dared to drop its acorns into the open field. Feeling as exposed as I was, I crawled through the opening, soaking my arms and legs in the process. The wind howled and the deer didn't see me as I planned their demise. When the right-hand deer turned its head I noticed a pair of small antlers. At only thirty yards, I guessed he was either a small eight-pointer or perhaps a yearling six. Lifting the bow, I immediately caught the attention of the doe on the left. Unsure what I was, she simply made two short bounds into the woods where she stopped, never looking back at me but now untouchable through the brush. The small buck remained a moment longer, glaring in my direction. *Now or never.* I drew the bow and before I reached full draw, the game was over. The buck disappeared into the woods in a single graceful bound. I watched helplessly as the pair walked back into the dark timber, certain they were heading calmly in the direction of my ladder stand. I hadn't spooked them badly and knew they hadn't gone far. There still remained hope for next time. And hope for next time is what it's all about. Springtime is not the only season full of promise.

Welcome to deer season.

14

THE BIRD FIELDS

WITH TWO early deer hunts filed in my field book of memories, I prepared for October's main event. That, for me, is bird hunting. I used to try to split my time unfairly between bird hunting and bow hunting for deer but it was an exercise in frustration. It never failed that we'd jump a large buck or see an impossible number of scrapes and rubs while pheasant hunting. It was hard to focus on birds, especially once the rut was under way, knowing my bow was hanging ignored from the garage rafter. And there were many afternoons on stand, especially within the frustrating confines of my home hunting area, when I sorely wished to be out in the field, covering ground and not feeling a moment's boredom while following on the heels of one dog or another.

When Max's first year ended with an unexpected number of birds in the freezer, especially for an inexperienced pup who never had other dogs from whom he could learn, I realized that I had on my hands an above-average bird dog. That winter I promised him to hunt more birds in October and less with the bow. I love deer hunting though. It took two years to finally come to the realization that time spent afield with the dogs was more important to me than bow hunting. With Max now a pro of three years, not quite in his prime yet but still a full-fledged flushing dog, I went hardcore. As hardcore as I could, anyway. I shot the bow a few times during the summer to keep up my chops, knowing that I'd want to hunt a few times, but I was firm in my resolution that October's focus would be bird hunting, and November would be dedicated to hunting whitetails. With the rut in our parts starting around November first and pheasant season ending shortly after that, there wouldn't be much overlap. I decided I could probably handle the pressure during those couple weeks of doing both. There are worse problems to have.

I cut my teeth hunting over multiple dogs but no longer have the luxury. Max, however, is the best of both worlds. With long legs he covers ground in a similar manner to a German short-haired pointer. His long strides are almost deer-like and the deep switchgrass is little impediment to him. Along with his athleticism and youthful energy, at the end of that hairy, golden body is one of the finest noses over which I've ever had the pleasure to hunt. The speeding, graceful bounds through the long grass don't prevent him from stopping on a dime when he picks up bird scent. I know the look. He pauses, furrows his brow, his ears come forward, and he is suddenly all shoulders and grunts, tearing up the trail of whatever he's discovered. Even for a flushing dog, he works very close, which has been a blessing for my wing shooting. When he's racing out of range, I know it is in my best interest to chase him down because some kind of bird is about to go up. Max seldom strays more than thirty yards from me so when he does, it's time to run. His retrieving skills, no thanks to my lackadaisical training, are also better than average. Max's first pheasant as a pup hit the ground alive and flew up in his face, terrorizing him. Still, he brought it back to me alive. I'm certain because of that first retrieve, two years later, he circles the birds with a suspicious eye before snatching them up. If they show any sign of life, he doesn't shy away, pouncing on them with a vengeance. He wouldn't win any field-trial competitions for form, but he never fails to get the job done. Max, shy and easily spooked by the rustling of plastic bags at home, has a bold hunter's heart.

Opening Saturday saw a limit of two pheasants, much to my delight. Much to my *surprise*, so did Sunday. And then Monday. Max had mastered ringneck pheasants. Maybe I was too quick to judge and this *is* his prime. My opinion has always held that a hunting dog's perfect age is five years old. Calm and experience has set in by then, but none of the lameness that inflicts big dogs far too soon in their short lives. *He's only three*, I thought after our third limit of birds. *Could he possibly get better?* I knew after opening day that my decision to focus on birds rather than deer, for now anyway, was the wise choice. There isn't a moment when I'm afield with dogs that I wish I were anywhere else. Scenery, often painted in the brilliant orange of the maples, flaming yellows of the ash and poplar, and the deep blood red of the dogwood brush, always passes by with something new to see. The leaves come steadily down, today revealing a hornet's nest in a tree I passed by a dozen times, making each return trip a unique experience. The beauty of fall is best experienced by burning shoe leather behind a good dog. I've known that as long as I have owned dogs. There's no schedule. If you want to sit down in the field and take a break, letting the dog have a drink from the water bottle in your coat while you scratch his ears and pluck some briars from his fur and tell him *good boy*, you just do it. There's nowhere else you need to be at that moment.

You're there.

Joy joined us for a pheasant-hunting trip that first week. Feeling ever so slightly guilty at the number of birds we took from around home, I decided it might be good to switch it up and head south a bit, to a large swampy area lined with switchgrass and bean fields. It was there that Max fetched and retrieved his first bird, and I hadn't been back since, so some *full-circle* action held more than a little appeal. The swamp holds a lot of pheasants and doesn't see many pheasant hunters anymore. The old farm fields, now overgrown with switchgrass and brush, are rutted, ankle twisting and frustrating. There's a reason that I rarely run into other hunters there. Even the grass seems especially thick, pulling at your legs and making your hips ache in short order as you try to high-step through the grabbing, serrated grass. It's hard on dogs, too. I hunted my springers, Maggie and later Charlie, here a few times but with their short legs it was an exercise in frustration for all of us. Maggie, later in life, nearly killed herself fighting through the grass after one particularly elusive bird that unfortunately turned out to be a hen, so I couldn't shoot it for her. I'm pretty sure she never forgave me for that. For Max and those lanky powerful legs, the place holds promise. The problem would be in Joy and me keeping up with him.

Sitting in the gloom of the daylight, misty rain speckled the truck window. We watched the digits on the clock slowly move toward legal daylight. When it finally arrived, I opened the back door and let Max out, telling him to stay close and asking him nicely not to start without us as we shucked into our hunting jackets and hats and I loaded up the old twelve-gauge. When the gun clanked shut on two fresh shells, Max was off like a shot. Several days of hard hunting had not robbed him of one ounce of enthusiasm. He was more pumped than ever.

It was tempting to walk the trail along the east edge of the sea of grass, but that would be taking the easy way. I offered

Joy the option to to stay out there, but she trudged behind me in the long grass, getting as soaked as I. The rain, at least, had stopped. She pulled her camera out, shooting some video and photos as the road dropped off in the distance and we were swallowed by the wild open land near the swamp.

Max was on scent within five minutes. I told Joy we were going to have a flush any second if she wanted to shoot video. Any second turned into five minutes, then ten. Max, no longer beelining to the south, looked confused. Racing around us in circles, he turned back to the north before heading south again. He rarely looked anything but self-assured when working scent but he paused by my side several times as if to say *what the hell?* I told him I didn't know and that he'd just have to figure it out.

He did.

Two rooster pheasants flushed only ten yards from us, a perfect seven-ten split as one veered north and the other one south. I dropped the right-hand bird in an explosion of feathers against the gray sky. As soon as I pulled the trigger on the second, I knew I'd been roughly a thousand feet behind him. I've killed a few doubles in my life, but this was not to be one of them. Not even close. I watched the bird and tried to mark where he landed, but at the same time Max was bringing me the dead pheasant and I lost track. A bird in the hand and all that . . . I was dimly aware that the second rooster landed in the cattails near the edge of the swamp. Considering that the cattails at the edge of the swamp spread for hundreds of yards, I could have marked him a bit better.

Joy stuffed the big bird into my game bag while I scanned the edge of the swamp. There were a few little points of cattail reaching out into the field and one small patch of brush. I tried thinking like a pheasant. *Where would I land?* Not pausing for pictures—*not yet*—I pointed Max in the general direction of the oval-shaped patch of brush two hundred yards to the south. If the bird *was* there the flush could go two ways. He'd either blast out over the field where he had already been shot at, or out over the swamp, resulting in a nasty, smelly swamp retrieve. Max would do it and I supposed he could always ride in the rear of a truck like a real hunting dog if he got covered in swamp muck.

Max read my body language, realizing that I was not hunting leisurely but rather waiting for him to perform. He knew I was headed somewhere and, after a couple of years of hunting together, had a pretty good guess that we were approaching a bird. Abandoning his normally close hunting pattern, he covered ground even faster. I had to whistle him back, realizing that he was trying to outthink me.

"You need me. Someone has to *shoot* that bird, Max," I said, making him *stay* a moment. I wondered what Joy thought of the man-dog dialogue.

Max didn't look convinced. I plucked a feather out of the corner of his eye, trying to assure him that *I* was calm and not in any hurry. A very smart dog, he knew better. He knew we were headed toward the escaped bird. After swinging back to give Joy a quick sniff hello, he took off again at full throttle toward the tiny brush outcropping. Giving up on the idea of controlling him, I jogged along, cursing the ruts and realizing that *I* was no longer in my prime either.

Max disappeared into the brush to my left, snorting. I caught a glimpse of the bird running down a deer trail just inside the tangled mess. Max was right behind it. Knowing he'd been had, the bird flushed impossibly close to me, towering for a moment above the cattails. It was long enough for a shot. When he dropped into the reeds, it took Max another moment to sort it out before emerging with the bird, his legs black up to the ankles in swamp water.

After posing for photos we hiked back to the truck, this time taking the trail, walking slowly and celebrating our success as the clouds gave way to sun. It was the fastest limit of birds in my history of upland hunting. The drive home only took a half hour. Max dozed comfortably in the backseat. Swamp muck or not, he'd earned the comfortable ride, though he'd probably have been as happy in the back of the truck so he could guard his pheasants. We were home for coffee before nine. *Maybe I should get out there and bow hunt*, I thought, since birds were off-limits for the rest of the day . . . *just maybe.*

Back home, the other two dogs mugged me as I carried the bird vest into the garage. Samantha, the lab who has hunted a few times but is at retirement age, and Lucy, our springer who was rescued from a life of being a backyard breeder, circled the birds. When I set the roosters down for the two non-hunting dogs to inspect, Lucy picked up the larger bird and trotted off into the yard with it as if she'd been retrieving pheasants her whole life. She was old, fat, and enjoying her post-rescue couch life, but I looked carefully at the little dog as I took the bird back from her. With her soft face, deep eyes, and liver-and-white coloring, she's always been Maggie's doppelganger. That's probably what made taking in a third dog so easy, though she had no hunting experience and I had no plans to hunt her. Watching Lucy with the pheasant, though, I couldn't help wondering . . .

A few days later, Lucy joined us for yet another lucky day of pheasant hunting. She didn't miraculously turn into the reincarnation of Maggie and didn't do much at all other than trot along with Joy and I, pausing to watch Max flush birds and racing along with Max in only a few short bursts to assist on the retrieves. Even when she found the noxious, muddy goo at the edge of an old irrigation pond and immersed herself up to her ears, emerging completely covered in black, I was glad to see a dog enjoying life the way a dog is supposed to. For seven years of her life, she only knew kennel life and I don't particularly care if she ever flushes a bird.

She's a part of the family, now.

15

THE GHOSTS OF PRICKER POND: PART I

I'VE NEVER killed a deer at Pricker Pond.

Each year, I scout, I hang stands, and I do all the things I've done at other places where I've killed deer with a fair amount of frequency, but I've never killed a deer at Pricker Pond. When I shot my first wood duck at Pricker Pond twenty-three or twenty-four years ago, it was truly a Pond surrounded by Prickers. There were only a very few places to access the pond without the tearing thorns and multiflora rose inflicting serious blood loss. Like most things, even Pricker Pond moved on and mellowed, becoming a kinder, gentler version of its menacing namesake. I don't think anyone used the name "Pricker Pond" other than John, me, and the owner. I'm not sure anyone else knows the place even exists, wedged as it is between old farmland and a nasty thicket, much less that someone who did know about it might have given it another name. Pricker Pond was a good a name as any, shortened usually to "Pricker" as in the text I sent Joy saying, "I'll be at Pricker this afternoon."

Though the area had changed in the last twenty years, little had changed since last year. A wall of dense brush facing me to the east, the pond and its smaller unnamed counterpart just ten yards behind me. To the north stands a tangled patch of willow and ash from whose brush piles I've shot many rabbits over the years. To the south lay a small strip of woods between my stand and the small, active crop field above, known only as the Goose Field in conversations between John and I. Too many sensitive neighbors around these days but, God, we had fun shooting geese there. I thought briefly of Ted. Smiles. Tears. The field, no longer planted in the sweet corn that the geese loved, now alternates between beans, cow corn, and ryegrass in the off years. Whatever is planted in it, the deer that call the thickets around Pricker Pond home are always drawn there. In my quick scouting of the area, checking on the condition and security of my hang-on tree stand, I observed deer tracks on all the trails. There's a main path between the thicket and the field with several lesser paths in and around the thick brush. The trail that sparks my interest every year is the tiny, twelve-foot patch of earth separating Pricker Pond and her little sister. It's a natural funnel, so choked with brush that it is not passable on foot. The deer have, however, for generations kept a small tunnel in the path open through which only they can pass. My stand is at the east end of the tunnel where the funnel intersects the trail out to the field. It's a classic deer setup—one from which I'm always sure I'll kill a deer.

After two decades, I still haven't.

I've shot a couple of trees with my handgun and one with the shotgun. I mortally wounded an apple tree several years ago from which I had a great deal of difficulty pulling the arrow that had missed a six-point buck by a small fraction of an inch. Other arrows have gone other places. Each year I've cleared shooting lanes but the nature of the cover around Pricker Pond is that in every direction there's a bad shot waiting to be taken.

It's thick.

I've watched countless deer pass at precisely forty yards on the far side of an old tractor path—one of the only truly clear shots in the area around the stand. My effective bow range is about thirty yards. I prefer twenty. Most of the good bucks I've seen have been broadside at forty. One of them, a huge, gnarly eight-pointer, would have been the buck of my lifetime. I return each gun season, certain I'll see a deer at the edge of that clearing where they were untouchable during bow season. It never happens.

The main problem, aside from the brush at Pricker Pond, is my stand. High in an ancient poplar tree, one in a long line of crooked poplar trees that sprouted up in an old irrigation ditch, it's the only straight tree (and not very straight at that). The poplar has only one side suitable for hanging stands, and it faces away from the place the deer usually appear in the afternoon. It's nearly impossible to hunt in the mornings due to the blinding sun obscuring the surrounding brush. With years of bad hunts under my belt at Pricker Pond I've learned to only hunt the stand in the evening or when I am certain it's going to be a cloudy morning. With that set of restrictions, I'm usually hunting there in the late afternoon and the deer, being deer, usually come in behind me and surprise the hell out of me. I try to stand facing west, hoping to catch a glimpse of their approach. Several times, I've detected light ripples on the smooth pond surface that were neither muskrats nor ducks, but deer sneaking along the edge of the pond. But for the most part they come in behind me, catching me off guard. This is what almost always happens at Pricker Pond.

The few times I've seen deer approaching in time to prepare, I've met with the aforementioned string of bad luck. I'm usually a good shot with the bow but not at Pricker Pond. As the stand faces the wrong way and there's a small secondary trail on the narrow strip of earth between my poplar and the pond, the deer frequently pass directly behind me. Almost all of my shots are taken while leaning out around the tree, stretching my safety harness to its very limit and shooting with what could only be considered *no form at all*. The results, and the broadhead scars on the trees around the poplar, are a testament to my lack of success.

A glutton for punishment, I keep coming back to Pricker Pond. It's no coincidence that it was my second bow hunt of the year. There are deer there. One day I will kill one of them but I need to do it soon.

More on that later.

There's other entertainment as well. There are plentiful rabbits that creep out of the brush piles right before dark, always there but only visible when there's a blanket of snow. They often hop around at the base of my stand. There's a red fox that frequently sneaks up the tractor path, stopping often to sniff the brush piles for the rabbits. The main attraction at Pricker Pond, however, has always been the squirrels. The fat gray squirrels are thick here, as are the red squirrels. They have running battles as the grays raid the single, old beech tree to the north, and return to their nests in the poplars with a beech nut or two. There is usually a red squirrel hot on their tail, chattering to warn them away from his beeches. It goes on all afternoon. A year ago the grays expanded a woodpecker hole in the poplar adjacent to mine. Now I'm subjected to them pausing directly at eye level with me before they retire for the night. Last year, I was amazed to see four of the fat grays file one by one into the hole entering what I can only assume must be the squirrel condo to end all squirrel condos. I frequently hear them talking in there as darkness falls, saying to each other whatever it is gray squirrels might say. *One of these days, that red squirrel is going to chase me for the last time, Bill . . . I hate those things. They freak me out!*

I love to squirrel hunt but I have a deal with the squirrels at Pricker Pond. They don't give away my location to the deer by barking when a deer is nearby and I don't shoot them. So far, the treaty has been upheld. Even the disagreeable, temperamental red squirrels that have ruined more than one hunt for me in other places here seem to abide by the rules. They're more concerned with terrorizing the grays than worrying about me.

Settling in to an evening hunt with very little time left after work, I stood facing west, watching the funnel and the tunnel and keeping an eye on the surface of the pond for telltale ripples. The squirrels were busy in the leaves below me. I counted seven of them at any given time working the strip of land between my stand and the pond. Still fresh into bow season, I had to stifle my jumpiness when movement in my peripheral vision several times ended up being gray squirrels gathering leaves for their nests prior to dark. The sound of their shuffling is, as any deer hunter knows, quite loud and has lulled many hunters into a false sense of security.

I could fill a book . . .

When the sun was just an orange globe halved by the horizon and barely visible through the dense branches to the west, I sat down and took my bow off its hanger in preparation to climb down. Between my outstretched arm and my chest, a doe's head appeared directly below and behind me. She, of course, saw the movement and snapped her head up, looking directly at me. *Game over, again,* I thought, completely incredulous that this deer managed to sneak up on me considering I'd spent 99 percent of the afternoon looking at the precise place from which she'd just emerged. Changing course she went back around the tree and to my surprise stopped at the base of my tree, no more than two yards away.

I waited. When she took a step forward, smelling my footsteps on the tiny path I'd cleared to the tree, I saw she wasn't alone. Another adult doe and a yearling followed behind her. When they passed into the opening I lifted the bow off its hook as gingerly as if it were a bomb. I knew immediately that I shouldn't have tried. I know better. *It's Pricker Pond, for God's sake.* My mom would call such a foolish move *borrowing trouble.* I remember the phrase well from my youth. And at Pricker Pond, there is no need to borrow trouble. It is in abundant supply.

The lead doe, a big deer, stood broadside for one short second and again looked up. With her eyes fixed on me, the doe snorted once and stomped her hoof to let me know that there was no way, no how that I was going to be shooting her or one of her family members that evening.

She was right.

In the tree next to me a squirrel purred quietly as the trio of deer bounded off into the woods to the north. Unsure of what he was saying, I could only guess it was, "Welcome back to Pricker Pond."

Reflections

Frozen mountain pond, late December.

Doe crossing pond, early season.

Whitetail buck bedded in thick brush.

Whitetail buck trailing a doe.

Whitetail does at a high ridge crossing.

Three generations of whitetail deer.

Another hunter going about his business: sharp-shinned hawk and mourning dove.

Days gone by with Maggie and Ted, the ghosts that walk with me.

Max, hot on the trail of pheasants.

Max and his hard-earned bird.

Whitetail buck in heavy cover.

Ringneck rooster pheasant in a grassy field.

Max putting the 'retrieve' in golden retriever.

A small reward after a long walk. Max with a woodcock.

Who knows what the day has in store?

16

STRANGERS

There are no strangers here; only friends you haven't yet met.
—William Butler Yeats

If a man be gracious and courteous to strangers, it shows he is a citizen of the world.
—Francis Bacon

WHEN MAX was just a pup (far too young to be retrieving waterfowl, according to the books), I shot a pair of Canada geese over him. One agreeably dropped on the grassy dike at the edge of the swamp. It was the same swamp where he recently flushed Joy and me a limit of pheasants inside of twenty minutes. But he was not experienced then, barely more than a long-legged, lanky rookie. The bird that crashed on the berm was promptly pounced upon with a great enthusiasm and shaking of feathers. When I pointed the second goose out to Max, floating belly up in the swamp, he looked at me as if to say, "No, that's okay, Joel . . . this one is fine."

Not wanting to turn him off to water retrieves, knowing it doesn't come naturally to all dogs whether or not they have *retriever* as an integral part of their title, I encouraged him by nudging him toward the edge of the water. He responded by walking away. Though Max had performed a handful of cold water retrieves on the sandy shore of Lake Ontario as a young pup, he showed no desire to step into the mucky edge of the Alabama Swamp to retrieve the goose.

Trying to lead by example, I pulled my fishing waders out of the oversized hunting pack and slipped them on before stepping into the black, sucking muck. I got within six feet of the bird when the soft bottom suddenly gave way to an unfathomable depth. I barely caught myself from going under. I reached the barrel of the old pump shotgun to within a foot of the bird but could not stretch it that last eleven inches. The slight breeze was the *wrong* slight breeze and it pushed the goose further out of reach. I was frustrated. Max showed no sign of the powerful water retriever he'd eventually become. It's hard at times like that to remember that your six-month-old pup is a *six-month-old baby.* I tried to remember.

Two shots roared to the east; there were other goose hunters nearby. I sat on the shore, peeling out of the black goop–covered waders, before swallowing my pride and walking east. The strangers' chocolate lab was retrieving a big gander. The young guys, no older than twenty, turned toward me and the forlorn golden retriever puppy now huddling timidly behind me, certain he'd committed some unforgivable sin by not retrieving our second goose. Walking up on people in a blind while the birds are flying is not recommended behavior and I was thankful when I was not met with harsh words.

"Hey guys . . . my pup is just learning and we have a dead goose in the swamp . . ."

I'd barely gotten the words out when the lab's owner said, "Let's go! Brandy, come!" After the short walk during which a few pleasantries were exchanged between the humans, the old lab spotted the white belly of the overturned goose. Performing a flawless retrieve, she even allowed Max to snatch the goose from her jaws once on shore. Brandy got a pat of thanks and a piece of venison jerky from my backpack. Max strutted proudly around my pair of geese as if he was the only one that had anything to do with it. Brandy's owner didn't stick around, eager to get back to the business of hunting. He accepted a handshake and was gone, saying only, "Just holler if you get another one." It was refreshing to see such a gesture in someone so young.

I've been privileged to hunt in many places private and public, lonely and otherwise. You can't pigeonhole hunters as *social* or *antisocial*. In reality we are just a cross-section of human beings everywhere. Some are polite and go out of their way to be kind, like Brandy's human. Some are jerks. I've met both kinds. Over the years I must admit the polite humans outnumbered the others, but when a true jerk is encountered, the overwhelming statistical politeness is easily overlooked.

When my circle of deer hunters was still regularly deer hunting in the Catskill Mountains, Steve rescued a lost hunter one day. By Steve's telling, the guy wasn't particularly friendly, but after hearing the circumstances of his lost-ness, he understood his poor attitude. It seems that he'd gotten lost while riding his ATV to his mountaintop deer stand. After losing himself, he walked away from the ATV to look for landmarks that might suggest a course correction. It wasn't long before he realized that he'd now lost not only his way, but also his very expensive all-terrain vehicle. Steve gave him a ride back to his camp, the location of which wasn't easily identifiable since the hunter didn't have the slightest clue where he was. When the lost hunter offered Steve some gas money, Steve refused and asked that the hunter just do something nice for someone else in the near future. In a time before *pay it forward* was in the lexicon, the hunter agreed to pay it forward. I keep wondering if there isn't a nice ATV still adorning some Catskill wilderness mountaintop.

I've encountered a lot of strangers during this lifetime of hunting. Duck hunting the public areas tends to be a social sport. I remember many dark mornings at Beaver Island State Park, waiting for the duck blind drawings with Jay and Tom and John. We made friends there, and we encountered people with whom we'd never *choose* to share a blind. Pheasant hunting the public areas sometimes becomes an exercise in civility—or not. Dogs have a way of treading on other people's cover. To me, it's the true test of a gentleman hunter whether he can accept a polite apology when someone else's damned dog over runs their cover or occasionally (I'm looking at you, every bird dog I've ever owned) rushes in to retrieve another dog's bird. The sound of a shotgun is a powerful tonic to any decent bird dog and it's hard to get mad at them for racing to Pavlov's gun. Some guys can laugh it off. Some cannot. Most of the hunters I've met, dog people to the core, can laugh it off. To those who couldn't? I've quickly forgotten their faces and the unnecessarily confrontational glares that were painted upon them in angry shades of red.

During my second return to the southern tier, after a wonderful afternoon of deer scouting and squirrel shooting, Max pounded the bean field where the early season rooster pheasant had made such an impression upon me. We worked the fields and the draws. Hunting the long grass and the tight brush of the creek bottoms, we killed a woodcock, but never once encountered a rooster pheasant. After four hard hours of hunting in the increasing October warmth, we paused back at the truck where I refilled the water bottles, ate a Pop-Tart and grudgingly checked my phone for work messages. Though I'd seen their truck parked on the far side of the road, I didn't notice the quartet of hunters approaching until Max's tail began wagging in the shade of the truck. He raced off to meet the family's Brittany while I brushed Pop-Tart crumbs off my hunting vest and stood to join him.

They were nice people, good people. Though no formal introductions were made, I learned they were from a small town just a bit to the east of my own small town, and that they'd never hunted here before. The youngest son pulled a fine rooster pheasant from his vest and showed me. He was no more than fourteen. I inspected the bird and approved of it as if he'd just handed me the keys to a safe deposit box containing a small fortune. In reality, he had. His mom and dad appreciated that, while his older sister looked away, too cool to be bothered. Nice people. Good people. They were the kind of people that when they walked away you would say, *Damn, those are some nice, good people.* When Mom and the kids began wandering back to the truck, the Brittany and Dad and Max and I talked a few moments longer. Walking the few hundred yards to simply say hello and pass the time was a small gesture on their part, but one that sticks with me. I hoped that own my kindness and the fact that Max wanted to go home with them would remain with them as well, especially the boy with the rooster pheasant. You never know when you've meant something to a stranger. Maybe you never have. Maybe I never have.

Let's keep trying.

I've been lucky enough to encounter some very good people in the field. The bad ones? Yes, there have been a few. There were a handful for whom the game laws were undoubtedly written for someone else. There were some who felt their dogs were too good to be rubbing shoulders with my poorly disciplined pack. Some are just rude. There's one in every bunch but, for the most part, the people that truly share a love of the outdoors—and an appreciation of someone *else* who holds dear the things that they hold dear—are all that matter. The world, especially the outdoor world, is full of good people. The bad ones? I don't give them much thought at all.

And, if you see me out there, please say hello. If you're having a rough morning in the swamp, Max will be happy to fetch your pup's goose.

17

OCTOBER INTO NOVEMBER

THE FLOWERS said it all.

One cold morning, I was on my way to work when I should have been on my way to hunt something, and it was garbage day in Lewiston. Trash totes and giant recycle bins lined the roadside in the growing daylight, an army of blue robots awaiting their orders. One raised its lid in thanks as the frigid autumn wind had carried it out into the road and I narrowly avoided sending him to the trash-robot afterlife, whatever that may be. Just before turning up the hill that would take me to the four-lane that would take me to work, one of the overstuffed garbage totes flashed briefly in my headlights. Three pots of chrysan-themums were tossed on top of the trash, two with roots up and one with its frostbitten yellow flowers reaching up as if to beg for just another few days on the porch. It wasn't to be. Just as certainly as those mums would soon be in the landfill, the celebrated month of October would give way to the misunder-stood and seldom appreciated gray of November. Sometimes I think only hunters love November. Everyone else I know thinks of November as a somber funeral for another year. For me it's the start of the most exciting time in all of hunting season. I do, however, mourn for October before diving headlong into the coming month.

Most people love October, even those that crave the summer months. For their own reasons, everyone is sad to see it go. My reasons vary. Maybe it's that October is so full of bird hunting and bow hunting and mountain trips. It is the first immersion into the heart of hunting season after the slow burn that is the squirrel hunting and equipment preparation and target shooting of September. September is a fine month. October, though . . . October lives in my imagination during the summer months. I never think much about November until it's on my doorstep ready to kick off the pumpkins that have gone a little too soft. October is fiery and red and bold and easy to love. During the summer, October daydreams are blue skies and flushing rooster pheasants and grass that crunches underfoot. When it finally arrives, October is so full and fast-paced that it is gone before it ever had a chance.

The flowers in the garbage can were a not-so-gentle reminder of how most people hate November. Our own mums were still on the porch, not yet destined for the mulch pile. Throw them in the trash? You have to be kidding me. They were keeping the softening pumpkins company and adding a splash of *real* autumn brown to the front stoop. It's not that I was leaving them there as a reminder of October. It's just that I'd been so busy hunting. By the time I tried to move the big rotten pumpkins, I had to get the wheelbarrow. Even then by the time I arrived in the backyard, I had little more than tepid pumpkin stew to pour onto the pile. The mums were next, their dry husks piled onto the mulch pile looking nothing like the radiant flowers of a few weeks ago.

November came on like it always does.

Winter painfully creeps away into spring. Spring eases into summer and if you don't bother to check the date on the calendar, there really isn't much difference between late spring and early summer. Summer eases into fall, a few yellow leaves mixing with the greens and a handful of cooler days. But November, the unofficial gateway to winter, has no such amicable period of adjustment. November kicks October out to the curb with a vengeance, treating it like yesterday's trash. One day you're pheasant hunting in late October and a few leaves have fallen and most of the trees have turned. The next day it's the weekend on the far side of Halloween and invariably some strong wind will bring a front in from the north and the one-two punch of rain showers and wind gusts vacuums the leaves off the trees as if they were never there. I've hunted the woods during these massive leaf-falls. It's always a psychedelic snowfall of red and green and orange and yellow. Deer trails disappear under the blanket. The hidden secrets of the woods are exposed and the deer stand that seemed far enough away from the road now looks as if you could successfully sell lemonade to passing cars by merely waving your arms. The transfer from October to November is a cutthroat business deal that is conducted during a single angry meeting.

October puts on a great show but November always wins the negotiations.

Pheasant season was still under way during those first few days of the new month and our luck continued well into November. Max showed no sign of slowing. I'd deer hunted a few more times with the bow, with several sightings but no luck. Pausing on the front porch after the memorial service for my own chrysanthemums, then dumping the mushy pumpkins out back, I looked to the woods across the street from my house. There's a stand there, too. Impenetrable and dense in the summer, the small wood lot eagerly gave up its secrets. With leaves pulled down, only bare branches remained. The outline of the small abandoned house at the end of the lane cut its usual silhouette back in the woods, now home only to raccoons and squirrels, and the occasional kid trying to sneak a smoke. During the summer you'd never know it was there.

I enjoy the coming of November and not just for the deer hunting. It's a different kind of love affair than the one I have with its predecessor. Unlike the temporary showiness of October, November is a natural beauty. The grays and browns are the permanent colors of nature. They're there through all the seasons, just dressed in different colors. The old stone fences that line the wood lots never waver in their moss-covered grayness, never feel the need to change. The gray trunks are the sturdy framework for the greens of summer and the colors of fall. Their job is thankless, but, unlike the leaves, you can always depend on them. They'll be here when you need them. November isn't a month of death, but a suggestion of what matters in life. It's a reminder that when the buds break out in the spring, and the leaves in the summer, they will have a place to live their short brilliant lives. The geese stop in only briefly on their way to places where the seasons don't mean such drama. November welcomes them, like the leaves, only for a brief time before they move on. November clears the woods so the deer can more easily follow their rub lines and perform their ancient breeding rituals. November removes the haze from the sky and the leaves from the trees for the lone hunter who keeps his flashlight off, preferring to find his way home by the bright beacon of the harvest moon. The geese are up there too, following the lunar light and honking their goodbyes. For all the hurtful words used to describe it, November rarely complains. Why should it?

November will be around long after we're gone.

18

HERE'S YOUR SIGN

I WAS racing home from work with my mind focused on nothing but the fastest possible route to my house and into the closet to get my hunting pants and pull them on while breaking open the gun safe. All of this would have to be executed with a very excited golden retriever who'd waited all day to hunt birds.

On the outskirts of town I slowed instinctively at the Free Methodist Church. That's where the thirty-mile-per-hour zone begins, and it's been a speed trap as long as there's been a church for the cops to hide behind. Not that I was averse to risking a speeding ticket in order to enjoy the last hour of daylight in the fields with Max, but because I frequently curse the people who speed through *my* thirty-mile-per-hour zone at the other end of town. I am averse to hypocrisy except when I need to be hypocritical, so I dutifully slowed.

At that point in time, this book was only a string of ideas loosely held together and bound by memories. The sign on the Free Methodist Church's front lawn, though, gave me pause. It simply said, "Don't Let the Ghosts of Your Past Haunt Your

Future." It was a reference to Halloween, and to something more.

In the field near the lake that afternoon with one woodcock and one pheasant in the bag, I thought about that sign and turned the words over in my mind. As I did, the ghosts were all around me, more present than ever. I didn't have to struggle to see their faces or hear their voices. Sometimes they walk with me. Sometimes they haunt me. Despite the sign's advice, I invite the haunting. Regrets are often magnified in the lonely fields of autumn when a dog is your only companion and not capable of saying much by way of consolation.

I had ideas for this book but, like a pile of unruly October leaves, I needed a theme to tie the pile of notes and words together. I always work better creating a title first. Maybe the message was from God, although it was likely just the ramblings of the associate pastor at the church, and as any good United Methodist churchgoer can tell you, the Free Methodists aren't likely speaking for God. I took the sign as a sign because there aren't many other ways to take a sign. *The Ghosts of Autumn* suddenly came to life.

Here's your sign.

19

MY KIND OF GUY

MY VOW to make October bird month and November deer month was well except for those few overlapping weeks. I was a basket case, not knowing until the last moment when I pulled in the driveway where I'd be headed. Would it be to the woods to the south, or across the road? Should I get Max out again for birds since the season is nearing its end? But it was deer season. I should be deer hunting. The whitetail rut *should* be under way, but despite the fact that the first of November had passed, I hadn't yet seen much in the way of rubs or scrapes or bucks wandering carelessly around during broad daylight in places they should not be.

During a few of those first inaugural days of November, it was easy. The deer seemed to be shut down, according to the reports I was getting from my bow-hunting contacts. It was natural to take Max for birds without any credible evidence that the radical change in deer activity had yet begun. We killed more birds.

Then, one morning, Max and I had a tremendous ten-pointer cross our path at one of the bird-hunting haunts. I followed his trail, discovering several rubs on trees as large as my arms, and a dozen scrapes in a hundred-yard patch of woods. On the way out a small buck was strutting in the waning daylight, pestering a small doe as she crossed the grass field near the road. Deer appeared where none had been. The rut was on. The reports came in from my small circle and my easy decisions suddenly presented more difficulty.

Max and I had a bountiful bird season, but despite the rut being *on,* it was hard to break away from the idea of open fields and endless wandering and commit myself to hours on the deer stand. I knew those hours could be punctuated by some of the greatest excitement a hunter can have, but still . . . it takes a certain mindset. A deer hunter's mindset is not necessarily the same as an upland game hunter's. No more than a duck hunter's mindset is the same as a turkey hunter, nor any more than a trout fisherman thinks the same way as an avid pike fisherman.

To have a love affair with more than one of these passions is to sometimes have to throw one of your babies out with the bathwater, at least for a while. It's possible to do both as I've proven for years, but it's a whole degree of difference to be very successful at both. I'd been successful at bird hunting in no small part due to Max the past couple of years, but my bow hunting had suffered. This was the year I was going to break the streak of bow-hunting misfortune that had plagued me more in the last two years than in the twenty-some-odd years I've been hunting with a stick and string. With the rut here, I knew that that magical time of hunting season that is brief, chaotic, unpredictable, and something I think often about in the off-season had finally arrived. Yet, I suddenly found myself not altogether willing to give up my success in the bird field and let Max retire by the fire for the remainder of the fall.

I was more torn than I've ever been during that subtle seam between October and November. Who did I want to be? Bird hunter? Bow hunter? Did I want to be James Bond, or John Rambo? Even that isn't a fair comparison. Did I want to be Sean Connery playing Bond, or Daniel Craig? Roger Moore? Different tactics, same results. There's something noble and fine about bird hunting that conjures up images of fine shotguns and good bourbon, sharp khaki outdoor clothes and well-bred dogs. There's a different mindset with bow hunting. It's equipment-heavy, secretive, deadly, and, given a little luck, a lot of heart pounding action and high-stakes adventure. Bruce Willis could easily be envisioned saying, "Yippee kay ay, Six-Pointer."

But who am I? As I pulled in the driveway, I still didn't know where I was going or what I wanted to be if I grew up. I walked past the garage where Sean Connery's upland jacket hung by the door. *Maybe.* Briefly breezing into the back bedroom, I checked out Rambo's camo outfit and ran my fingers over the smooth lines of the compound bow that had, until recently, put an awful lot of venison and bear meat in the freezer.

Who would I be today?

20

THE CAPTURE

I'VE BEEN a photographer longer than I've been a fisherman, and far longer than I've been a hunter. My crowning glory as a kid was photographing a pair of great horned owlets when I was eleven years old. One of my first great woodland adventures was being dive bombed by a pair of great horned (full-grown) owls while photographing their cute, fuzzy babies. While I didn't suffer any permanent scarring, one of them managed to knock my hat off and both of them put the fear of God into Monty, my first golden retriever. I still have those photos. From those early wildlife photos, I gradually blended the love of photography with my love of fishing. My first fly-rod trout was recorded on a twenty-four-exposure roll of two-hundred-speed film on a crappy little point-and-shoot camera. My *last* fly-rod rainbow was recorded on a slightly better digital camera that I still dare to pack in my waders after drowning several cameras. One of them was not at all crappy nor cheap. My first squirrels are recorded on Kodachrome 64 slide film and the colors to this day are better than anything I've ever shot on digital, despite an ongoing pursuit of new technology. Most of my deer hunts have been photographed, though there was one mercenary weekend in my youth when I killed five deer to help some of the old timers in my circle fill their freezers for the winter. I didn't record any of the bloodshed. Most of it, though, has been memorialized on film. If you've hunted with me for any length of time you're going to end up on film or, more recently, stored on hard drives.

Images are powerful. Like my predecessors at Lascaux Cave, I have the overwhelming urge to record all that has happened. It's annoyed more than one hunting partner. My close friend Jay frequently complained about the photography done in the duck blinds when my Ted hunted alongside his Jake. They were both stout and powerful black labs and both photogenic as hell. When Jake had retrieved his last duck and went to that place where all good dogs eventually go, I presented Jay with a photo of the glory days: Jake, young and strong, standing at the edge of an ice shelf on the bank of the Niagara River, a limit of bluebills spread out before him, the ice tinted with the colors of blood and feathers. It was a moment in time that we would never have again, but thanks to the camera, we always will.

Jay didn't refuse the photo.

For a long time, John had a harsh view on the photos. Being an artist, he appreciated the work but often lamented that they'd end up in some shoebox only to be thrown in the trash a generation or two later. In his mind, my kids would invariably say, "What are we going to do with this *crap*?" I disagreed with him and I think he eventually came around to my way of thinking. It's okay to be sentimental, to hold something tangible in your hands and see your younger face looking back at you, and to say, "I remember that day."

John's cynicism aside, I shot photos of almost every hunt we ever had together. There aren't many hunts I don't have filed away in an album or, in the past decade, on a CD or on a hard drive. I used to make a point of getting prints made. Remember prints? Whoever I hunted with got a package of photos from me. Joe, chest-deep on Grass Island in the pre-dawn deep freeze of the Niagara River, got photos even though I didn't know Joe. Marty in the Upper Peninsula got a set of photos. Andre, when we bear hunted in Maine. All of my local friends are up to their ears in prints of the old days. I don't care if they end up in a shoebox and if their kids eventually throw them out. Possessing those photos to have and to hold and to *remember* meant so much to me that I always made sure that they were well distributed.

We're in a different era now.

I still take hundreds of photos each hunting season. Sometimes thousands. When I retired my last good digital camera, it had seventeen thousand photos on it, and the camera that replaced it is already racking up an impressive number. Gone are the days of expensive prints and enlargements and processing. The digital world has been a blessing to those of us enamored with capturing a moment in time.

It has also been a curse.

Instead of printing out photos and handing someone an envelope of four-by-six glossies from some special day afield, now all I have to do is pull the memory card, insert it in into my computer, spend a minute or two on Photoshop and send them on their way. Digital photography has opened up a world to us photography enthusiasts that is so immediate, so *easy*, that it's almost destroyed what those boxes of photos stashed in attics and waiting to be discovered meant.

Even in the old days film was expensive. To shoot a thirty-six-exposure roll of Kodachrome meant seven or eight bucks in film and another five in processing. And if you wanted to get prints from those transparencies, big bucks. Now? I can shoot thirty-six frames of Max retrieving a pheasant and it costs me *zero*. If I want I can shoot a thousand pictures of a pheasant hunt, delete the nine hundred I don't want and it costs me nothing. Even the cameras are cheaper. What's also cheaper, though, is the experience. If you go bear hunting with me during the last week of August, I may shoot a few dozen photos of the north Maine scenery, a hundred or so of the moose we see on the way to the baits, and maybe another two dozen when you get your bear. I'll email you the best ones.

But then what?

You'll forward them to a few friends, maybe put them on Facebook or whatever the cool kids are using as of the publication of this book. Unlike those prints that might end up in a photo album or even a in a simple box in the linen closet, or stashed in the attic, the lack of permanence infects them like a computer virus from day one. I'm not overly morbid, but I sometimes think of John's shoebox-to-trash scenario and realize that digital photography has put the future of our memories even further at risk. For the most part, there won't even be a bunch of photos to find when I'm gone, other than the few I have framed on the wall. Who will bother to go through my hard drives and backup drives and CDs? What are CDs? For many years I backed things up on those shiny discs that seemed so full of promise in their permanence, but now computers have already started coming without CD drives. Maybe in the future, the CD will be as retro and cool as vinyl records right now, but I somehow doubt it. The late-'80s technology already seems antiquated when you can put several thousand photos on a small SD card. And twenty years from now? Who knows what the medium will be. Maybe someone will come up with some futuristic turntable that plays CDs, but I think that prints are going the way of the *Megaloceros*.

Joy and I recently stopped at her uncle's house after a successful pheasant hunt with Max. An avid hunter, one of the first things Uncle Jud did was bring out his photo albums and let us pore over the pictures of bucks and successful coon hunts, and rows of foxes hung on the side of the barn after a stellar trapping season. There were coyotes and pheasants and dogs and dogs and dogs. Other than the greenish hue of the aging prints, the albums may have been my own. And then I realized that I stopped putting photo albums together almost ten years ago. That gave me pause. Most of my stuff would never be printed now. There's really no need for it. Right? I'm not so sure.

So what? So what if those photos are gone. Live in today, Joel, right? Enjoy those photos on the wall and scroll through those years of photos squirreled away on the hard drives. Relish looking back at the things that meant something to you. Maybe there will be no great void when all of those hunting and fishing and wildlife photos disappear forever into the ether. Maybe it's good to not saddle the next generation with a bunch of faded memories that really only meant something to you.

Wait just a minute, says I.

I want those photos to be around for my kids and their kids. I want them to see Maggie and Ted's last hunt—a photo whose significance I didn't even realize until a year after they were gone. I want the next generation to see the five-year-old Jessica posing on the back of a nice Catskill spike buck I shot with my old Bear bow. I want Jennifer to remember the day she stood in the shed next to a huge eight-pointer that had been taken that morning in a miserable rainstorm and had required two strong men and an ATV to get it hung by the rafters. I want my kids to see what Dad and Papa and the boys were up to way back in 2001. In that batch of photos also reside photos of their direct ancestors tearing up the Catskill hillsides, dragging deer and smiling goofy deer-hunting smiles for the camera in the rain and mud and snow. There are bloody hands, and sweaty faces and autumn leaves and green hillsides. Captured in those photos is the excited gathering of friends during that magical time known as hunting season. The fun was captured on film. It's as simple as that. The photos are history, not just my history, and I want them to live on beyond my own life. Is that so selfish? I'm sure that the artists in Lascaux, who undoubtedly enjoyed their own work, had an eye toward telling their story to future generations. That's only my speculation, of course, but I would like to think so.

My daughters have inherited my love of photography. Jessica, my oldest, has rebelled against the digital storage trend and gets her photos printed. She often gives me an envelope with prints just as I used to do with my hunting partners. Despite being born and raised in the computer age, she still gets prints. There is a simple beauty in that. You don't have to turn on a computer. Hell, if you want you can just use a magnet and stick them on the fridge—*old school.* It's a trait to which I can relate. Joy recently inherited boxes of ancient family photos from another uncle. The faded sepia prints are a doorway to generations that are long gone. The photos remain as touchstones for the memories of the people that have gone before us. The worth in that is incalculable.

I've no intention of giving up digital photography, but maybe it's not too late for me to start a shoebox.

21

THE RETURN

We are all travelers in the wilderness of this world, and the best we can find in our travels is an honest friend.
—Robert Louis Stevenson

JOHN HAS been my friend almost as long as I've been hunting. He's been my hunting partner for 99 percent of my hunting career. I started hunting in the late '80s and became friends with him in the early '90s. We've killed geese, ducks, coyotes, foxes, deer, squirrels, rabbits, woodcock, pheasants, and I'm sure some other prey which at this moment escape my mind. I introduced him to the joy of hunting the Catskill Mountains for deer. He introduced me to duck, pheasant, and woodcock hunting. His were the first dogs I ever hunted over, which started my lifelong love affair with four-legged companions. There aren't many people that end up in the same workplace and are as enamored with fly fishing and hunting as John and I; it was meant to be. He started off as my boss but we were destined to be friends.

For all of our similarities, we are not the same. John is a people person, outgoing and loud and fun. I'm a writer, quiet and not as open with my thoughts, except when I'm alone with a close friend or a blank piece of paper. In other ways John and I are blood brothers. We're silly, sarcastic, and no matter what the circumstances, always looking for a good story in whatever happened to us that day. John expresses himself in verbal story-telling and painting, while I let loose in photographs and words on the page. He's outgoing at the spur of the moment while I'm only outgoing after I find a way to present my experiences once they've percolated and settled and formed into words that I can share with others. We're very much the same, and very much different. We've disagreed on a lot of things that have come up in our quarter century of friendship, but we'd defend each other to the bitter end. I don't know that either of us would call the other his *best friend* but I know for certain that John is one in a million as far as my friends go. If I need someone to be honest with me and tell it like it is, or to fall back on when the shit hits the fan, I've no doubt that John will always answer the phone. He knows that I'm similarly there for him. In that way, with all of our disagreements and banter and bullshit, we remain good friends.

And now he's gone.

John, my boss, friend, fishing partner, hunting partner, confidante, fellow musician, and all-around sarcastic bastard, retired to Florida last year. I wasn't sure my life would be the same. When I moved from hardcore bow hunting into hardcore bird hunting, John and I switched places. A quarter of a century ago I was the diehard deer hunter and he, the duck and pheasant hunter. I introduced him into the world of precision archery, while he immersed me into the wonderful world of dogs and birds, ducks and bourbon, and Gene Hill's books.

Now, all these years later, John is the master bow hunter while I am the guy who picks up the phone to tell stories of birds and dogs. John's last dog was Minnie, a fabulous yellow lab now many years gone. John joined me for many bird hunts with Max, and when an arrow flew, he was the first person I called to help me take up the blood trail. I don't know how many times we've helped each other track deer. Dozens, at least. Last year I was just finishing a bird hunt by the lake when my cell rang and John let me know that he'd just arrowed a nice buck. I only paused at home long enough to drop off Max and pick up my flashlight. John had known that the shot was true, but he still let me in on the short tracking job that led us to a fine seven-point buck piled up just inside the woods, its belly white against the darkening November night. There was back clapping and handshaking and photo taking. I knew John didn't need me as soon as we found the deer, but I also knew that *he* knew that it's a good thing to share the experience with a friend who had taken up the trail with him on so many other occasions that had not proven so easy.

Aside from the countless pheasants and woodcock and ducks, John and I had taken up the trail of so many deer that I can no longer remember all of the stories. There's the eight-point buck I shot on the last day of deer season many years ago which was complicated by the *doe* I'd shot a few moments earlier. The tracking went on for twelve hours in the nasty thicket, testing our skills. Both deer ended up in the freezer and one on the wall (he's looking at me right now). There was John's second Catskill buck that he swore he'd hit on the left side and had gone north, when in actuality he'd hit it on the right side and it had gone south. There was John's liver-shot eight-pointer that went eight hundred yards, my single-lunged doe that went two hundred. I found it the next morning after sacrificing a vacation day and calling John at work to tell him the good news after we'd searched for it all night. So many deer. Though I can no longer remember all of the stories, trust me when I tell you they are countless. John would drop everything to help me find a deer and he knew and still knows that I would do the same. It's an agreement on which we've called each other a million times over the years and never has either one of us come up short in the help department. We've lost a couple of deer over the years but never for a lack of trying.

When John announced his retirement to Florida, I couldn't begin to tell you how that felt. He'd lived only a few miles from me for all of my adult life, and he was the one constant in my small circle of hunting friends. *When a deer runs off into the night*, I wondered, *who will I call*? For all of our disagreements and differences, John was the one person who, without fail, would show up with his cell phone, flashlight, and just the right dose of, "Calm down . . . we'll find it," for his nervous and anxious friend when the deer blood hit the fan.

Our duck hunts together ended long ago and John's passion for upland hunting ended with the death of Minnie. He still joined me for one or two hunts a year over my dogs but that's never the same as running your own mutts. He did it more or less to humor me. Our main social activity in the last few years has been deer hunting. No matter where opening day finds us or how we divide up the time during the season among other places we've been individually invited to hunt, we have never failed to get together to hunt deer during the gun season.

When John returned for several weeks that spanned the middle of bow season and the beginning of gun season, he hunted like a madman. I couldn't help wondering if he was feeling pressure to get back at me for all of those trout, woodcock, and pheasant photos to which he'd been subjected so often in his email inbox. If his plan was to get even, he executed it perfectly. In almost no time he'd sent me a photo of a doe he'd arrowed in the Southern Tier hills. Not long after, I stood in our mutual friend's barn admiring the massive eight-pointer arrowed on another friend's property. After that, another doe. My texts and emails were soon full of John's trophies. I couldn't help but laugh in between bouts of jealous admiration.

On the very last night of bow season, rustling in the leaves near one of my little-hunted bow stands revealed a deer moving quickly through the brush in my direction. The light was dimming and I willed the deer to come closer. Buck or doe, I didn't care. I was ready to make a bow kill. It had been a long, long time. When the deer emerged at the edge of a small clearing, I waited with more patience than I possess for him to clear one small sapling.

Just one more step.

I put an arrow into the chest of the small six-pointer. While the sun set on my stand, snowflakes began to fall and I listened as the buck crashed off into the dense brush to the east of my stand. It was snowing more heavily now and the blood trail would quickly be covered. That fact gnawed at me. I was also wary of the nasty thorn thicket into which the deer had disappeared. Before I could even climb down, darkness enveloped the woods around my stand. I pulled my facemask off and snow nipped sharply at my cheeks. Fishing around in the pack, I dug out a flashlight and headed toward the thicket then paused, thinking better of it.

I always rush it.

The snow had me worried. Adrenaline coursed through my veins and I knew from twenty-five years of doing this that the decisions I was making might not necessarily be good ones under the circumstances. Trailing deer, I'm adept at being the voice of reason for other people, but when it's *my* heart rate that's elevated and *my* blood pressure that has reached dangerous levels, I know that I tend to jump the gun. I've made more than one poor choice that ended up in a long night of blood trailing.

Only one thing to do.

Digging my cell phone out of a protected inside pocket, I called John. He was at a welcome-home dinner party and spoke to me in hushed tones. I heard voices all around him. His advice was sound. "Go for it before the trail gets covered up." It's what I would have said to him. I thanked him and was about to disconnect when he added, "Let me know if you need me, and I'll be there." I smiled in the gathering gloom, searching for the blood trail in the yellow beam of my light. It didn't take long. I was on the trail in only a few moments. Blood glistened on the sides of saplings and in small sprays in the trail. I thought I heard the deer crash out ahead of me in the dark and I paused, wondering just how well I'd hit it. Of course, it could have been another deer.

Kneeling in the thicket and dousing my light for a few moments, I caught my breath and tried to relax. I'm pretty good at tracking deer. If I'm not *good*, I am at least determined. *I can do this*, I told myself. While I was trying to calm my nerves despite the increasing wind and snow, I spotted a flashlight beam bobbing in my direction many hundreds of yards away.

It was John.

I flashed my light in his direction and he quickly covered the distance. There was no debriefing, no storytelling. I pointed to the last pool of blood. The quiet between us was not grim, but hopeful. We knew what to do. We didn't need to talk, but John played cheerleader to my nervous gloom-and-doom. Had it been the other way around, I'd be trying to cheer him up as well, saying *I know we'll find that deer* even on the long, dismal trailing jobs when there was little hope of *finding that deer*. We'd been here before.

It's what friends do.

22

DEER SEASON EVE

ALL THE pheasants that would be shot this year had been shot. All the woodcock breasts that would be eaten with toast and eggs had been eaten. A handful of squirrel and pheasant tails were stashed away in a coffee can by the window with care, in hopes that some flies eventually would be tied there. All the hunts of the year had culminated in this glorious, snowy "Deer Season Eve."

I paced the house. I piled my gear in the great room under the quiet supervision of several deer heads and bear rugs. I got the feeling they weren't rooting for me, but I've grown accustomed to their scornful stares. I'd packed and unpacked my backpack a dozen times despite the fact that it had been packed a month ago for Nobleboro, packed several times since for varying bow hunts, and I knew precisely what was in each and every pocket. There were no mysteries hiding in the secret corners of the well-worn pack. This was not the same as Equipment Time, which came and passed much earlier in the season. This was different. This was the night before deer season. I laid the items out just once more. I put fresh batteries in electronic gadgets that probably had fresh batteries just two weeks ago. I wanted them to have fresh batteries *again*, damn it.

The weather tomorrow would be cold. Frigid, even. And there might be snow. I moved to the heavy duffel bag and packed and unpacked my waterproof coveralls and parka, checked that I'd crammed some dry underwear and socks in the outside pockets. *What to wear, what to wear?* I decided on a suitable outfit. It had to be light enough to wear on a substantial hike up into one of the areas I'd marked during squirrel season, yet warm enough to protect me once I'd worked up a sweat from hiking too fast. John's legs are longer than mine and hiking with him is *always* an exercise in, well . . . *exercise*. For good measure I threw another pair of long johns into the bag that, despite the amount of gear already packed, seemed to have unlimited capacity. It wouldn't be until I struggled to move the bag to the truck later on in the proceedings that I'd realize just how much clothing was stuffed into it.

It is the clown car of duffel bags.

Next I picked some clothes to wear for the drive. I couldn't wear hunting clothes for the two-hour ride into the hills; I'd sweat too much and eventually stink. Besides, it's hard to drive while dressed like the Michelin Man. The driving layer had to be easy to shed in the dark by the side of the road. It would be cold—ten degrees last time I looked at the forecast. Being half naked for very long on the road side would not only prove visually unappealing to those who might pass by in the early pre-dawn hours, but might also cause frostbite before the first hunt of deer season even began. I chose carefully.

Once the pack was packed, the duffel bag was duffeled, and a suitable driving ensemble was assembled, I set about the fun part of the night. Opening the long-gun safe as if I were an archaeologist opening a long-sought tomb, I selected the only gun that I could select. Though other deer guns stood silently in the shadows, there really was no choice. The Winchester Model 70 that had served me so well on countless deer and bear hunts leaned out of the shadows. In recent years I'd killed deer with shotguns and handguns and bows and muzzleloaders, but it had been a long, long time since I'd hunted in rifle country. The last animal I'd killed with the .30–06 was my last bear, and that had been almost five years ago. Before leaving the safe door I worked the bolt, its slick action well broken in from years of field use and countless kills. A heavy rifle, its weight was a comfort. The rifle said, "I've been waiting for this." Maybe that was me. I'd periodically checked on it during the off-season, frequently shooting imaginary bears on the wall of the back bedroom. I sprung it from prison a few weeks ago for a range trip to make sure it was as deadly as ever. I hadn't any doubt, but was still thrilled when it punched paper in tight groups. The Winchester is to my big-game hunts what my double shotgun is to pheasant season.

Back in the great room I sat on the floor next to the fire, next to the duffel bag and the backpack and the cooler full of sandwiches that Joy had prepared for John and me. Peering down the barrel with my gun light, I was dazzled by the spiral grooves. After running a clean patch down the bore, I wiped away the excess oil. Pausing before stowing my number-one rifle in its case, I held it for a while before swinging upward at the big bear rug and then down to the smaller bear that had been my last trophy, now permanently posed above the fireplace. They didn't appreciate the display, but there wasn't much they could do at this late date. It was too close to see anything other than a black blur through the scope, but for a moment I was back in Maine. I then swung upward to my big Catskill seven-pointer, the last deer the rifle had taken—too many years ago—and for a moment I was on that high, lonely hillside sharing the day with friends. John and Steve, Mike and Howard. The rifle, really just a piece of simple machinery made for shooting bullets, was for a moment a gateway to days gone by. I placed it in its case, wary of its time-machine properties. It wouldn't be the first time it transported me to the past, but I had more work to do before I allowed myself to spend too much time with the ghosts of autumn. Tomorrow morning, deep in the woods of the southern hills, I would welcome their company. Tonight, I had to keep moving. After one more check to make sure I didn't forget the bolt and the scope covers, I latched the case, putting the rifle back to sleep for just one more night.

Opening the small safe in the closet, I looked over my rifle rounds. There were three boxes of .30–06 shells I'd had for twenty years or more, with a round or two left in each. The boxes were beaten and tattered, their rounds tarnished with time. I didn't select them. Nostalgia lost out to a pair of newish green-and-yellow boxes which I cracked open to see the fresh, bright brass and gleaming copper-jacketed soft-points. I tossed the new Remington boxes into my duffel in a place of prominence on top of the extra clothes.

I wanted to kill a deer.

Opening day used to mean an excursion to the Catskills for Steve and John and me. There used to be a big *night-before* build-up to our hunts, often with a party. Stories and exaggerations and sometimes even the truth about past seasons were remembered. We paged through photo albums and often watched old videos of our hunts from the early '90s at Doc's farm in the Catskills. Doc is gone now, and it's been years since any of us hunted the mountaintop farm that provided countless memories, hundreds of pounds of venison, the occasional wall mount, and a never-ending supply of laughter. After our last Catskill trip together, our small group started falling apart. Steve went his way on subsequent opening days while John and I still tried to hunt together on the opener for old-times' sake. Eventually, John and I had our own places to celebrate the rising sun of opening day and the circle was broken. The last few years, however, we made it a point to *at least* get together on the big day, both acknowledging in our own ways that sharing the sacred sunrise of the first day of hunting season was something that should be done whenever possible. Shortly after John's return from Florida, he suggested that we hunt together opening day, and I suggested the place I'd discovered during squirrel season.

There was no party as in past years, but as I put the finishing touches on my pack and my duffel and the pile of clothes for the drive, I imagined John doing the same, preparing for tomorrow. I was certain Steve was also going over his pile of gear with German precision and organization at this very moment, preparing for dawn at another friend's hunting camp. Porter would be on his way home from school about now, getting excited for the coming morning. Before bed, wishes of good luck came in from my small circle of friends in the form of texts and phone calls. While not the same as a "Hunting Season Eve" party, it still somehow seemed appropriate. I had no desire to try to replicate the party atmosphere because, I realized long ago, the party and the anticipation are all in my head, and everyone else would be celebrating alone in their own way as well, packing and preparing, dreaming and hoping. That is celebration enough.

There is rarely a day hunting that is as wonderful as the dreams of what it may be the night before. Before something happens, anything can happen. Therein lies the magic. Would this season live up to the anticipation? Bird season certainly did. Perhaps deer season would wind up a dreadful failure.

But tonight, on Deer Season Eve, anything was possible.

Unzipping my backpack one last time, I was elbow deep in the mess of hunting gear when Max curled up on the carpet next to me. Having endured several deer seasons now, he knew that the preparations were not for some far-flung bird hunt. There would be no feathers to cough up for a long time. Still, he shared the moment with a deep sigh and a shallow wag of his tail. Being one of the smartest breeds (as he often reminds me), Max knew that bird season was over for now and that deer season had begun. He resigned himself to his quiet months at home, happy for me (I think) in my excitement, which must seem, by bird dog standards, quite boring.

With my hand on Max's golden mane I looked at the pile of deer hunting gear and turned tomorrow morning over and over in my mind. The ravine I discovered during squirrel season blanketed in just the right amount of snow would be the perfect place to welcome the cold November dawn. I closed my eyes and visualized deer coming up the brook.

Once again a child on Christmas Eve, it was a long time before I slept.

23

OPENING DAY

WE'D ONLY just settled and the cold was already bone chilling.

The hike in by the light of the moon against the white carpet of snow was easy. We'd barely needed our flashlights, using them only as safety beacons and as a courtesy to any other hunters already hidden in the woods. Making good time to the distant ravine, we had walked perhaps a bit too quickly. As always, it was a challenge to keep up with John's long legs; we covered the distance to the place I'd hoped to hunt in much less time than I thought we would. By the time we crossed one ravine and a high oak ridge, passed through the huge golden-rod field, and dropped into the quiet confines of the steep, dry creek bed, I had worked up a mild sweat. Finding the twisted old apple tree with multiple trunks that I'd marked on my GPS all of those months ago, I settled in and took a deep draw of the cold, mountain air. It was the first truly frigid morning of the year and though I'd carried my outer layers instead of wear-ing them, I was still damp with sweat from the hike. The only solution was to take my extra long-john shirt from my pack (not my first time at this rodeo) and stash the damp one. If I left my damp one on, I wouldn't make it for an hour. It was simply too cold for any other option. That, of course, meant stripping down to bare skin while sitting in the snow with the temperature dipping into the single digits and a stiff morning breeze blowing across the snow from the dry creek bed below. Superman would have been proud of the speed at which I changed from damp to dry, naked to clothed. Zipping my parka over my fresh change of clothes, I nestled into the base of the old apple tree. Despite the speedy arrival, our timing seemed just about right as dawn broke on the eastern horizon, a thin strip of yellow edging away the starry night.

I tried to settle in. John, having never hunted this piece of land, took my advice to travel west down the ravine and take up a position above the junction of two creeks about two hundred yards from me. As the sun rose, though, I realized he was very close—less than a hundred yards from me. At the time I didn't know if he did it on purpose but I doubted it. He probably stumbled around in the dark for a while, thinking he'd covered more ground than he actually had. No matter, he was on the same elevation as I and we both only had one safe direction to shoot. That was down into the creek bottom. I had a doe tag and John did not. If a deer came out near us it could get interesting, especially if it was a doe, but I had full faith we could pull it off. We share the utmost trust in each other's safe shooting. Besides, John was in a relatively open spot at the base of a large beech tree with a somewhat better view than mine. I was in a more secluded area with only two shooting lanes but better hidden than he. The odds of either of us shooting a deer were about even.

With shooting light near, a flashlight beam bobbed below us in the creek bottom. Not surprisingly, the light paused for a moment as the person got their bearings and then switched directions, heading directly for my hideout in the apple tree. Someone else had obviously done their homework in the off-season as well. My heart sank. On the way into the area well before daylight, many trucks were parked on the sides of the road in this remote hunting area. Several groups of men, orange pumpkins illuminated by our headlights, were huddled around tailgates, sharing coffee and excitement. It was a public hunting area and I expected to run into some hunters on opening day of deer season, but the sheer numbers surprised me. I'd figured my advance scouting and willingness to get in away from the roads would protect us from the majority of the traffic. But there came the flashlight. John, a veteran of public hunting areas, had not been surprised at the numbers. Digging my own flashlight from an outer pocket of my pack, I signaled the incoming hunter, waving it in several arcs over my head. The light retreated back through the ravine, finally disappearing up and over the opposite side. Not wanting to ruin someone else's morning, I was nonetheless relieved. The hunter had undoubtedly left a suspicious scent trail in the very creek bottom in which I hoped to take a deer this morning. It was brutally cold and my hands were feeling it already. Also, with the growing daylight I realized that John was even closer than I'd originally thought, but as light oozed into the woods all around me, I focused only on the positive and let the negativity blow away on the frigid morning breeze.

In the distance, the first shots of opening day roared across the surrounding hills. Several solitary shots echoed as people got their deer very early in the season. One round of multiple shots erupted from another hunter presumably not having such success. At the present moment, he was probably looking for more shells. I smiled, my face cracking in the cold, and thought, *Been there done that.*

Movement through the brush on the opposite side of the ravine didn't startle me as much as it should have. It first appeared precisely where the wayward flashlight had been just before daylight, and I wondered if the hunter had gotten turned around and was heading back in my direction. But there was no orange and it took my brain a moment to realize that the accompanying cracking and snapping of twigs could only be a deer. The doe came into and out of my view faster than I could get my rifle up. I don't mind shooting a trotting deer but this one was moving as if on fire and I was relieved I hadn't the chance to pull the trigger. I could just make out the bouncing white flag as it angled past John and continued on up the ravine at breakneck speed. Peering out of my hideout, I craned my neck far enough to see my hunting partner. He gave me a quick glance as well, reading my mind. He pointed to the opening from which the doe had emerged.

Watch.

With my rifle up on my knee, ready, I watched the doe's back trail, hoping that a buck would be coming along behind her. I sat like that for a very long time, only stealing a glance at John who was my mirror image in the exact same position look-ing in the exact same direction. I couldn't help but smile. If a buck stepped out I had no doubt it would sport matching holes. Years ago on the last day of the season, John and I stumbled upon a lone doe as we walked and talked across a long-grass field. Shooting at precisely the same instant, we killed the deer, though to this day the debate rages on about who hit and who didn't. There was a hole in her ear and one in her shoulder. I'm fairly sure which one was mine, but then again, so is John.

I already loved this place. The ravine is much like the ravine on Doc's property in the Catskills where I killed my first deer and where so many other deer fell to our bows and guns that I can't even begin to remember them all. As the sun crested the far ridge and lit the snow-crusted trees in the amber light of morning, I thought about Doc. I remember the last time I saw him, during the early bow season many years ago. Ravaged by Parkinson's as long as I had known him, he was on his bed in the big house on top of the hill. His voice, barely a whisper, was thin and weak and he had pulled me close to the bedside. I strained to hear him but when he whispered into my ear the words were clear as a mountain brook. "I've spent a lot of time looking at these beams." He gestured upward with his eyes. I followed them up to the rough-hewn rafters of the ancient farmhouse. I'll never forget the twinkle in his eye as he displayed his wonderful sense of humor one last time. Years ago I'd written about what those woods and hills had meant to me, and when my writing was complete Doc was the first person with whom I shared those words. I try to be social but if you want to know what I'm feeling you might have to wait for the book. That said, I've always tried to tell people what they mean to me while there is still time to do so. I was able to thank Doc in his healthier years for his hospitality and to share with him the spell that his property had cast over my entire life. For that I am thankful. I held his hand for a long time until he drifted back to sleep.

I never saw him again.

The woods here are much like those on Doc's mountain—rugged hills and quiet brooks, big boulders and open meadows, old apple trees and scattered hemlocks. Closing my eyes, I pictured Doc's smiling face and the place I called my hunting home for two decades. Glancing to my left toward John, I remembered all of our adventures at Doc's property on Dahlia Hill. As if sensing my thoughts, John smiled in my direction.

Seven a.m. gave way to eight. Eight hadn't yet moved aside for nine when movement across the ravine again caught my eye. An older gent, so fully decked out in orange that I would have been surprised if his socks and underwear weren't orange as well, moved with a halting gait up the opposite side of the valley. Seemingly oblivious to my orange coat and John's own orange clothes farther down the valley, he continued on past us. Mildly frustrated at the intrusion, I kept telling myself that this is what I should have expected when hunting a new piece of public land. The hunter moved from our left to our right before disappearing into the split in the ravine near John. I shouldn't have been surprised when I spotted the deer sneaking back on him, having been the victim of such whitetail tactics myself many times, but I was. Ducking low, the deer appeared in the foot tracks of the recently departed hunter, stepping briskly in the opposite direction. Crossing quickly to my side of the brook, she kept her head down, cutting away from the trail the hunter had taken. She didn't realize that she'd stepped into an equally hazardous situation. Trotting for a few yards, she paused in front of John. I stole a glance at him. Exposed out in the open, he tucked his head down inside his coat as if that would hide him just a bit more. The deer was no more than twenty-five yards from him and stopped broadside directly in front of him. I felt bad that I hadn't offered for him to fill my doe tag if the opportunity arose, but at the same time, his deer hunting luck had already been far better than my own, so I didn't feel *that bad*. John played his cards perfectly, remaining motionless as the deer began moving again in my direction. When the doe disappeared behind a large stand of saplings, I propped the Winchester up on my knee. When she moved behind a single large hemlock, I snicked the safety forward, pulling my glove off with my teeth.

I'm not sure if she caught a whiff of John or heard the muted click of my safety but something suddenly alarmed the deer and she trotted several yards forward. She paused with her shoulder shielded behind yet another large tree. I could have taken a head shot but I didn't want to. *Not yet.* She made two quick bounds in my direction but again stopped behind a deadfall. I tried to play it cool but had been close to squeezing the trigger several times. My heart began to pound. Unbelievably, she took another short, panicky bound and landed again in a position that did not present a shot. This time she looked back in John's direction. When she took another tentative step forward, her body language told me that she was about to vacate the area.

Unlike a bad shot, a good shot seems like the most natural thing in the world. I barely remember the crosshairs touching her shoulder as she stepped from behind the last tree. I don't remember pulling the trigger. Only twenty yards away when the rifle roared, the doe dropped and slid a short way down the steep ravine, leaving a bright red trail in the snow. The shot was good and there was no need for a follow-up. Still, I watched through the scope. This wasn't the place or time for amateur mistakes and I wasn't about to make one.

Her death moan, a note of finality against the silent woodland morning, reminded me of three of the bears I had killed in Maine who had announced their demise in a similar manner. It's fair trade to be reminded by your prey that you've killed a living being, and a powerful thing to hear another creature cry out in a death that you delivered. I wasn't saddened, but allowed the doe's mournful cry to reach in and touch the thing that makes me human, glad to know that I hadn't become too cold-blooded after all of these years of killing deer. A small victory. Checking the time, I was surprised, and not that it was only nine. I again glanced in the direction of my hunting partner. With both hands, John motioned emphatically downward. *Stay put.* Though I wanted to run down to the doe, I stayed put, if only for a little while longer.

A few moments later, John met me at the doe and we both commented on her death cry. John imitated it, but without his customary humor. I was glad to see that the deaths we so often are tempted to take for granted still affected him well. It's not the kind of thing you're likely see at the climax of a carefully edited television hunting show. No high-fives. No hooting or hollering. Not here. Not today. Real life. Real death.

"Let's haul her up by your tree," John suggested.

We did, leaving a longer crimson trail in the fresh snow. Before we gutted her, John snapped several photos on my phone. Just before I unzipped her, I sent the photos to Joy, Steve, and Porter. Before I had finished cleaning out the big doe's plumbing, I'd gotten replies from everyone, the phone's quiet vibrations loud in the quiet woods. John only helped as long as it took to get her mostly gutted before returning to the base of his ancient beech tree. Feeling a little ridiculous, I placed an extra orange knit hat on the doe's head, insurance against a stray shot from one of the hunters sharing these woods taking a stupid shot at a doe lying on her back near a hunter clad in orange. If nothing else, the hat made me feel better.

John was back in position, scanning the ravine below us and hoping something else would come along, but we only hunted another half hour before he started back in my direction. He was smiling when he arrived, again placing his hand on the big doe's flank, patting her in appreciation.

"What do you think?" he asked.

"I think I'm really glad we came here."

"I am too. We should have come here last year."

I'd suggested it, but I stayed silent. That's not always easy for me. John understood the silence and smiled.

"Let's get her out of here," he suggested.

I told him no. I was ready to hunt all day and if we got another deer we could start dragging sometime in the afternoon to make sure that we were out by dark.

"Are you sure you don't want to drag her out?"

"No. Let's stay. I want you to get a chance. The day is still new."

"I'll make a deal with you," John said. "Get her home and hang her up. I'll help you drag, but you've gotta promise me that we'll hunt again this evening."

"Pricker Pond?"

"Pricker Pond."

We took turns dragging, with the odd man out carrying the guns and packs. Once out of the ravine, we were both startled by another hunter who had remained concealed in the shade of a hemlock as we approached.

"Great, you guys. Nice job." Young guy. Nice guy.

We thanked him and talked for a moment, John engaging him in the way in which he is so adept at engaging everyone while I gasped for breath from the grueling drag. My hunting partner and social butterfly filled in the gaps. The young hunter hadn't seen anything. The conversation was quick, as he was anxious to get back to his hiding place, as full of opening-day hope and anticipation as I had been for the past two hours.

Back at the truck both John and I were exhausted from the drag, having shed most of our clothes down to our sweaty final layers. Once at the road, I hiked the remaining distance for the truck, driving back to a small opening in the woods where we horsed the doe across a deep ditch and up onto the cargo carrier. An SUV with two orange hunters slowed and inspected us with frowning faces and deep scowls, never bothering to roll their windows down to say hello or ask to hear the story. Apparently they were not raised correctly. Either that or they'd had a really bad morning. I didn't mind. Not everyone has learned the code. I thought quickly of the guy in the shade of the hemlocks and decided that his kind words were enough for this quiet morning. The other guys? I forgot them before they rounded the next bend. We strapped the doe down and sat for a moment by the side of the road. John was gasping for air now too. It had been a long drag.

"What a great morning," he said, clapping me on the back before double-checking that I'd tied the deer down securely. "Let's get home so we can get back out there."

"Pricker Pond? Really?" I asked, running my fingers through the doe's fur.

"Pricker Pond."

24

THE GHOSTS OF PRICKER POND: PART II

IN THE afternoon, with only a couple hours of daylight left, I dropped John at my ladder stand and hurried into the stand at Pricker Pond. Down the muddy ATV trail, I tried to ignore the fresh deer tracks in the black mud, but I couldn't. Those new tracks in the soft earth near my tree stand frequently lull me into a false sense of hopefulness about killing deer at Pricker Pond. I knew they were there. I also knew that my chance of killing one—especially on a day that had already seen success—was less than zero.

At the poplar tree, I hung my forty-four magnum revolver from the lift rope and scaled the tree steps as quickly as possible in my bulky clothing. I stepped onto the small metal platform, strapped myself to the poplar, and lifted my revolver. Loading it as quietly as possible from the stash of fat brass shells in my pocket, I gently closed the cylinder and settled in. I wasn't as comfortable as I'd been in the hills earlier that morning. My inner layers had become soaked with sweat from dragging the deer out, and the outer layers sported a fair amount of blood and deer hair from unloading the big, early morning doe and hanging her from a beam in my garage. My backup, second-string clothes weren't as comfortable and, more importantly, they weren't as *lucky* as my number-one, go-to deer-hunting clothes, but I tried to relax and be hopeful regardless.

For opening afternoon, there was a surprising lack of shooting in the area. My hometown flatlands are not a hot bed of deer activity, unlike the hills to the south. Yet, the area sports some of New York's biggest bucks, especially on the lake plain. Even though the bucks aren't plentiful, there is a good chance of seeing a true giant if you *are* lucky enough to encounter a deer. Of course, that hasn't stopped me from shooting small bucks in Niagara County. The number of years between my two largest bucks in my home county would make you laugh. Trust me. Still, I was surprised there was *no* shooting, and I wondered if the morning had been just as dismal.

For a short while I faced backward, looking over the small strip of earth between my stand and the pond. With the leaves mostly down now I could see much farther, almost a hundred yards into the thick woods beyond the pond. Small parts of the area were obscured by tall cattails; I knew that it was from those areas that a deer was likely to emerge, and that they'd be on top of me before I was ready.

Welcome back to Pricker Pond, I thought, knowing at least that with my revolver I stood a chance against the pond's bad luck. Like the shotgun and the rifle, the big handgun rounds out the top three lucky firearms in my collection. It's never failed me, though I've failed it a few times with cold hands and rushed shooting. My problems aside, the revolver is responsible for my biggest buck. The act of carrying it inspires confidence. Last year, after a long drought, opening day came and went with one doe crossing a large grass field, passing me at eighty yards. I'd practiced with the revolver out to one hundred but did not take the shot. On the second day of the season, I'd steadied the handgun on the metal rest of John's ladder stand. When she came out again at precisely 7:20, I put the small red dot on her shoulder. She was so far out that the dot covered almost her *entire* shoulder but when I pulled the trigger, the revolver roared and the doe went down. On my way to recover her, I paced it off, at better than ninety yards. The shot had been dead on. As I said, *confidence.*

Back on the uncomfortable seat, I turned my back to Pricker Pond, knowing it was not a good idea. I was tired from the morning hunt and drag, and from hanging the deer. My back was hurting so I hunkered down into the collar of my backup parka and tried to get comfortable. A half hour before dark the wind settled down before dying off completely. I was positive that I'd hear any deer approaching from the rear. As always, the red squirrels were chasing the grays along the edge of the goose field. Other than that, the only sounds were of cars passing by, far up on Ridge Road.

I sent John a text, "Nice afternoon."

"The whole day's been good," he replied. Had that been the end of the day, I would have been satisfied.

That wasn't the end of the day.

Thinking ahead, I wondered where I had stored the meat grinder last fall. I wondered if there were enough vacuum bags to process the venison. I paid scant attention to the shuffling leaves between me and the goose field. I had never seen a deer approach from that direction, and the squirrel wars were under way last I looked. Glancing up from my daydreaming, I was shocked to see a line of deer coming down from the field. They must have crossed the road, and to do that in the daylight on opening day of deer season, something or someone likely pushed them. Still well out of range and screened by thick brush, I watched them. There were at least three. Once inside the woods their heads swiveled as they nervously watched their back trail. They were spooked, probably by a hunter leaving the woods early as dusk approached. Maybe a big buck was following them. I didn't think so. Something wasn't right.

The woods exploded with cracking branches and snow flying off saplings. Deer were everywhere. In retrospect, I think there were six but it might have been seven. Their numbers weren't important but their travel direction was. They made a break for the tiny tunnel near Pricker Pond, the same hidden pathway from which I've watched so many deer emerge. It made sense that they'd use the thick passageway as an escape route. Wherever they were headed, they were going to wind up behind me.

Naturally, *it's Pricker Pond.*

Standing quickly, I was uncomfortably exposed in the open woods of winter. There was no time for subtlety or stealth in my movements. I stood, spun to face the pond behind me and pulled the large revolver from its holster. I almost forgot to turn on the red-dot scope and when I remembered, my gloved fingers slipped on the small, slick knob. Yanking the rag wool glove off with my teeth, I barely caught it as the deer crashed past me. Most of them went not through the secret passageway but right *into* Pricker Pond, splashing through the knee-deep water and sending up geysers twenty feet in the air. Bringing up the rear was a small buck. Sometime during the fray I had cocked the forty-four. I don't remember doing it. I had the buck in my scope long enough only to see a lightning-fast brown blur before he was gone. I would've just as gladly killed a doe as the small buck but I never got a chance to pull the trigger. I lowered the hammer, then the gun, flabbergasted. The farthest of the deer had been no more than twenty yards away but like a herd of zebra, they had safety and confusion in numbers, aided by the splashing water spectacle as they quickly crossed the pond and disappeared into the brush beyond.

Before I had a chance to bang my head on the tree at once again *almost* killing a deer at Pricker Pond, the woods above me came alive again and a lone, large doe materialized in the tracks of the first group. Unlike the first bunch, she moved at a steady trot, not a panicked run. My revolver came up as if on a string and I steadied it against the tree trunk. Slowing as she approached the stand, she knew something was wrong. Stealing a glance up toward the field, I checked one last time to verify there wasn't a buck in hot pursuit. When she paused in the small strip of real estate between my stand and Pricker Pond, the red dot illuminated her shoulder and the forty-four magnum roared. The doe hit the ground hard and made a sound identical to the doe I'd shot just seven hours earlier. A short final moan, then silence. Even without the lonely ravine, even as cars roared by on the road above the goose field, the low cry put a lump in my throat just as it had in the morning. *This is the price*, I thought, but only for a moment. Climbing down when the doe was finished, there was only elation and surprise. I hadn't expected two deer on opening day.

The doe had gone down wedged between two large boulders. I had to drag her a short distance to get in position for field dressing. The motions were automatic. I don't know how many deer I've rolled on their back and opened up, feeling their waning warmth against the cold air while I set about the bloody business of gutting. But with my knife poised just above the big doe's chest, I stopped. A dawning realization came over me. *This was my very first deer from Pricker Pond.* I couldn't stop smiling.

Checking the western horizon with the sun now perilously low in the woods. I wanted to document the moment but there was no time to get back to the truck for a camera. I settled for a quick smartphone picture. *Better than nothing.* Texting John, I told him to stay put and hunt out the daylight. Compared to the long morning trek and dragging job in the hills, the distance back to the barn where we parked was short and I could easily get the deer out myself. It was nearly dark when the gutting was done. I gathered my pack and heavy coat and brought them halfway out then went back for the doe. I don't know if it was the tiring morning or just that it was one big, fat deer, but the drag was not easy. When I got the doe as far as my backpack, it was pitch black. I was tired. John was out of the woods. Cheating, I hiked to get the truck rather than drag the deer the rest of the way up the ridge to the barn. Darkness surrounded us and John looked as tired as I felt as we checked out the second deer of the long day.

"I know what you'll be doing tomorrow," he said, clapping me on the back.

Once the deer was hung, with my garage resembling something of a meat locker, I went in the house to tell Joy the day's stories. Later, I sneaked out once to admire the matching pair of deer hanging in the frigid air. My bones ached with the pleasant fatigue of a fine day spent outdoors. A fine *opening* day.

It wasn't long before sleep found me.

25

POSSESSION AND RENDERING

THE RENDERING started early Sunday morning. I planned to hunt all weekend, but with two deer on my hands I needed to get working. While not exactly a labor of love it's nonetheless a labor of respect and, despite the amount of work, is something I enjoy. I learned to skin deer from several of my hunting mentors, eventually putting that skill to use with one friend in his taxidermy shop and another in his deer-processing facility. I was younger when I had those side jobs and, at five dollars a deer, I learned to skin efficiently. While my skills have faded, I haven't lost the ability completely. I hope I never do. The rendering is just another part of the hunt. Once the work is done and the blood is washed away and the meat is packed into the chest freezer, often at the end of a very long day, it is a satisfying way to put a punctuation mark on the end of a hunt. It's a dirty job, and I feel like I should be the one to do it. One more way to show reverence.

When the doe sneaking up the ravine fell to my rifle, she became my responsibility. When the other deer took her last steps on the bank of Pricker Pond, I fully took possession of her. They were mine now. They would live in my memories, and this was my last gesture of respect to them. I stood between the two big deer, their fur ruffled unnaturally from the struggle to get them strung from the rafters. Eyes that were clear brown orbs yesterday were now sunken and gray. I thought only briefly about the previous day's success. *Time to get to work.* Lacking the imagination to make a more profound choice, I started the first deer first.

Processing a deer is like any other linear process. As with most things in life, explaining it is one hell of a lot easier than doing it. There's a beginning, a middle, and an end. There's more than one way to skin a deer and I've tried a lot of them. None of the methods are easy. There's a tactic that seems to have had a resurgence of popularity lately, at least on the Internet. Simply put, you skin the deer down a bit and place a rock (or another small, sturdy object—I've used a softball) under the hide at the high points (depends on if you've hung your deer from the neck or from the hind legs). You wrap a rope around the rock, and then you attach the rope to a piece of moveable machinery like a truck, tractor, lawnmower, or ATV. Then, you just pull the skin off. Just like that. No problem. Angels sing and your work is done. It works. I've done it.

But it doesn't *always* work, and therein lies the problem.

If the deer is warm, the method works pretty darned well. But even then, preparation is everything. The legs need to be sawed off, and the rear hams need to be skinned up far enough so you don't pull the meat off during the grisly tug-of-war. If you tug too hard or too fast, you might wind up with a two-hundred-pound carcass slamming to the ground, or worse, landing on the vehicle. And then there's the rock that suddenly pulls through the hide and flies wildly in the direction in which it is being pulled.

Ask me how I know . . .

I experimented several times, since abandoning the motor-
ized version and settling for the simple, tried-and-true tech-
nique of a sharp knife and a few good tugs. It's controlled and
requires no more preparation than the rock-and-truck method.
There may be a little more back strain involved, but you won't
bend your bumper or blow the transmission out on your all-
terrain vehicle.

Sawing the lower legs off the deer, I placed them in my
ice-fishing sled. With eight lower legs stacked in the sled like
furry winter firewood, I made the first cuts around the hindquarters. Slipping the knife along the front legs next, I zipped
them from knee to chest, and pulled a bit of the chest hide
down with them. The Pricker Pond doe, shot several hours later than the first, skinned more easily. Abandoning the knife for
a moment, I tugged the hide downward over the hips and torso.
I did the same for the second deer. I carefully worked the sharp
knife through the tailbones of both deer. More pulling and the
hide slipped down to the front legs. They took a little more
work and a lot more pulling. Soon, both hides slumped to the
tarp covering the floor and my two does hung before me. The
venison glowed red in the fluorescent lights. I sawed the heads
free and wrapped them inside their hides. Everything went
into the sled.

My hands grew cold, bordering on numbness, and I worked
more quickly.

Two coolers waited for the quarters. I sliced off the shoulders, still amazed that such powerful legs are attached only by
muscle. Next, I worked the backstraps down. I wished John
were there to help. I've done more butchering than he, but John
cuts a much neater backstrap. I got them done, pausing only
briefly to duck inside and warm my cold, meaty hands by the
fire while Max and Lucy sniffed relentlessly at my pants.

Next, I fished the delicate tenderloins out of the rib cage. The four of them would be consumed in the next two days. There is nothing finer than fresh venison tenderloins, and these would never see the inside of a freezer. I wondered absently if there was enough red wine in the cupboard to accompany the delicacy. Moving on to the final step, I carefully worked the knife around to the small ball joints of the hind legs. Freeing them, I caught the huge chunks of meat as they detached from the connecting joint and lowered them quickly to the coolers, their sheer weight threatening to send them plummeting to the bloody tarp.

Finally, I removed everything left on the carcasses. Working swiftly, I pulled a few more handfuls of meat from the rib cages, tossing them into the cooler with increasingly numb hands. Satisfied, I closed the coolers and set them out in the snow.

In the side yard, I chopped the ribs and other assorted parts into manageable pieces with my splitting maul and put them onto the ice-fishing sled as well. Taking a quick excursion into the woods by my home, I placed the parts out in the woods for the coons and foxes, coyotes and crows. It's another tradition. I hate the thought of one piece of useful meat ending up as just another few inches of landfill. This is the ultimate in recycling. Nothing would be wasted and by spring there wouldn't be a trace it was ever there.

Halfway done.

In the evening, I brought the coolers into the house to begin the butchering while Joy prepared bags for the vacuum sealer. As I progressed, the bowls for the ground meat began to fill up. As they did, Joy ran the grinder, mixing in pork and packaging as she went. Separate trays held roasts and steaks as I worked at the seemingly endless supply of quarters, even though there were only eight. The backstraps were last, cut into thirds for warm-weather grilling.

The house smelled of meat and we were both tired. The butchering that began at nine in the morning was finally completed at nine in the evening. Everything was packaged and sealed and labeled and finally carried down to the basement freezer. Exhaustion had crept in, helped along by a few glasses of good red wine (the correct choice for pairing with red meat, and there was one hell of a lot of red meat that evening). My last step was taking the cleaned bones out to the woods where, like the rest of the carcasses, the local omnivores and carnivores would further clean them. I dragged the sled, this time by the light of my flashlight, depositing the bones in another section of woods. With plentiful coyotes in the area, I was sure most of it would be gone by morning.

Back home, I leaned the sled against the fence where I'd wash it out the next morning. I draped the tarp over the fence as well, and stacked the coolers up in the garage. It could all wait until morning for cleanup. Or maybe noon, since I had some more hunting to do in the morning. Deer season can be a harsh mistress . . . Looking up at the night sky where constellations revealed themselves one star at a time, I was tired yet strangely at peace. Possession had been taken and the rendering was complete. I gave thanks in the frigid air one last time for the two opening-day deer that now would always be mine.

26

MONDAY'S GHOSTS

I DIDN'T think I'd shoot a deer the next time I went out. Tempting fate and the deer hunting gods, I returned to Pricker Pond on Monday after "Opening Saturday" and "Rendering Sunday." The deer gods laughed, probably wondering why I was trying to shoot another deer only a day after spending twelve hours butchering. I'm not sure I knew myself but then again, I did.

Morning passed at Pricker Pond with nothing but the usual squirrel fights and rabbit sightings. When I climbed down to pick my way out of the thick cover, I was tired. I hate to admit it, but I was looking forward to a few hours on the couch before the evening hunt. A new layer of snow covered the bloody drag marks from Saturday evening, and fresh deer tracks were everywhere. I crossed the small loop in the ATV trail and stopped, stealing a glance back at the tree stand, still well concealed against the large poplar trunk even in the sparse woods of November.

And then I heard a snort.

Behind me, not forty yards away, a deer bolted. Branches cracked and the dark form vaporized into the thick brush to the north. The deer had been there the whole time I'd been on stand and only broke cover when I stopped. Breaking my way through the thick saplings and nagging thorns, I found the bed. Within sight of my stand, the deer-shaped depression was melted deeply into the snow cover. The deer was hiding just a few yards away and probably watched me climb into the stand. Niagara County deer are nothing if not bold. Imagine the nerve. The deer could've been a fifty-pound fawn but, in the interest of torturing myself, I prefer to imagine it was a huge buck, corn-fed and barely able to carry its obscene antlers through the woods. I still-hunted out of the thicket, resisting the urge to stomp my feet in childish frustration. I may have stomped once or twice by the side of my truck before heading toward the warmth of home. I don't recall. *Pricker Pond*, I thought while driving. *Pricker freaking Pond.* The sentiment was not new. For twenty years, the place has caused similar outbursts. After finally killing a deer there, I figured I'd need to save up another twenty years of luck before I could pull off a similar feat.

The afternoon found me high on the ladder stand that I'd risked life and limb to secure all those months ago. I wasn't hopeful. I wasn't watchful. In the last two hours of daylight, after fulfilling a promise to myself to relax for a bit at home, I was simply putting in my time. It was deer season and I had to deer hunt. No other options were available.

Settling into the ladder stand near the fields where I'd learned to be a hard worker, there was nothing on my mind other than thinking about how nightfall would be a welcomed blessing. A nice glass of wine or bourbon, a comfortable pair of sweat pants, and the gentle tapping of winter snow against the window would provide a respite from the hard hunts on Saturday and the hard work on Sunday. My back ached from the dragging. My hands ached from the skinning. Just tired in general,

I was more than ready for a break. I love to hunt but I'm no longer a twenty-year-old guy. I figured I'd earned a breather. About an hour before dark, however, the hunting gods lit a small fire under my tired posterior.

The revolver pressed heavily against my chest and the holster strap cut into my shoulder through the insulation of the heavy parka. My feet, cold from too many hours of inaction on the stand, were beginning to numb. Scanning the woods from left to right, more out of a sense of duty than any real hopefulness, something seemed off to the south, at the edge of my vision. I'd looked over this same stand of saplings during bow season and during crossbow season. For the last two hours I kept busy reacquainting myself with the oak stand. Yet something was out of place. A small lump of brown just a touch over a hundred yards away appeared where it should not have been. Thinking of the binoculars in my backpack, I decided to remain motionless. It wouldn't be the first time that a stump or log or bush assumed the appearance of a deer and with a brain already tired from a month of hunting and two days of hard labor, I wasn't about to believe anything my eyes told me. Besides, if it *was* a deer, it was far too close for me to stand up and fish around in my pack. Too much movement in too tight a space. Not a good idea, especially now that the deer were spooked from two days of gun season.

I wasn't surprised when the brown lump of log stood up and turned into a deer.

I'm an optimist. I always think or hope that the guy I run into bird hunting will be a *nice* guy and want to shoot the breeze for a few minutes. I like to think that every time Max gets excited, there's a woodcock or a pheasant flush coming—not just a field mouse or a wood rat. When I saw that small deer stand up, for a few long moments I was sure it was a big buck. A monster, no less. I'd seen big bucks in the woods adjacent to my old tomato-picking haunts and once even missed one there. A huge deer was not out of the realm of possibility. I couldn't have been more surprised when it started in my direction. Picking here and there at the underbrush and pawing the snow aside to get at the newly fallen acorns, it was in no hurry. I couldn't have been *less* surprised when the big buck transformed into a very small doe. Opening week was full of does.

I'd have been ecstatic with a small doe had this been opening morning. It wasn't. Two does were in the freezer and my supply of doe tags was exhausted until the late muzzleloader season, so I sank back into the confines of my heavy parka and watched her come. The trail I'd discovered in the summer leading out to the bean field hadn't been heavily used since deer season began, but this one was following the old tractor path past my stand as if her destiny had always been to do so.

Thirty yards from me, broadside, she paused and looked calmly in my direction. There was no real need for concern, apparently. Wary of a buck coming along behind her, I watched her back trail, but she had been bedded alone and no buck appeared. Putting on a show for the better part of twenty minutes, she pawed at the snow and vacuumed acorns, and at one point almost bedded down. With sunset almost upon us, I quietly pulled my camera out of my pocket and shot some video of the small doe feeding around my stand. I couldn't have asked for a more cooperative subject. She finally moved on to the northeast, passing the spot where I found the downed ten-pointer before the season, pausing briefly to sniff its skeleton, now encased in six inches of snow. Working eventually back toward my stand, she passed within twenty yards of me before making her final turn out toward the bean field. Darkness was near, and she would be fully concealed by the night.

I watched her out there, a faint silhouette through the saplings at the field's edge, finally just a black shadow against the
snowy landscape. When she was well away, I climbed down
and headed for home.

27

FALLBACK WOODS

THE NEW tree stand I hung in the woods near my house three years ago has served me only slightly more unsatisfactorily than my stand at Pricker Pond, and that's only because I *finally* killed a deer at Pricker. The hang-on stand, high (too high) in a beech, overlooks a field corner. Nestled in a small patch of good oak woods, it also has a good view of a small branch of a Lake Ontario tributary where I used to catch frogs when I was a small boy, and in which I fish for steelhead now as a considerably larger boy. During the (usually) quiet fall evenings in that stand, it's not uncommon to hear the salmon splashing up through the narrow gravel runs. In the early season, I've left the stand prematurely more than once to fetch my fly rod.

I've seen deer from that stand, but more often have bumped them on the way in. It's not been without entertainment value, however. From the high perch, I've watched coyotes, hawks, and owls, and one evening was entertained by a family of red foxes teaching its pups to catch mice in the long-grass field, but getting deer within shooting range continued to elude me.

Eventually, after a season and a half of poor luck, it became my fallback place. If I got home too late from work in the afternoon to make it to another, better place, I would take up the high stand in the field corner and hope for the best.

Typically, the stand's best wasn't very good, until one late afternoon last November, a couple of weeks into the rut. With salmon splashing in the nearby creek and squirrels chasing each other up and down my tree, skittering past me at regular intervals and just generally aggravating me, I put my time in on the fallback stand. With all of the other distractions, including the growing desire to make the short walk home for my heavy fly rod, I barely noticed the deer emerging from the far edge of the field. A small ditch reached from that opening in the woods, 280 yards away, to directly under my feet, and the area was thick with deer tracks. Unfortunately, when I finally bothered to set a trail camera near the stand, I realized that almost all of the deer activity near the stand was nocturnal, explaining my utter lack of luck despite the plentiful sign. Suddenly the doe was there and I realized there was a good chance she'd cross the field and come within handgun range.

With the big doe angling directly toward me, my heart rate crept up. Before she'd made it ten yards into the field, however, a small buck raced from the edge of the woods and cut her off. Even at two hundred yards his body language was clear. With head slung low, careless jerky motions closely resembled Max on fresh pheasant scent. He dogged the doe. She wanted to be rid of him. He turned her away from my stand and back toward the far woods. I watched helplessly, my fingers wrapped around the revolver's rubber grip so tightly I could feel my pulse in the palm of my hand. Before the small buck managed to herd the doe back into the woods from which they'd come, another buck broke out of the cover fifty yards to their left.

My breathing hitched. My heart skipped several beats.

The monstrous buck stormed into the field and the smaller buck vaporized as if he'd never been there. Both buck and doe paused. I carefully lifted the binoculars from their hook. He was as nice a buck as I've ever seen while deer hunting. Possibly the best. *Probably* the best. His huge body was twice as large as the adult doe that, ten minutes earlier, I would have been happy to shoot. From that distance, I confirmed ten points. Each of his tines was high and when he turned sideways, his rack clear against the dark backdrop of dogwood brush behind him, I gasped at his width. With a high, bright rack with thick bases and beams that extended far beyond his ears, I was in awe of the Lake Ontario rim monster. He was simply a classic, huge buck, a true wall-hanger by anyone's standards. I began thinking about finding a place for him on my wall. Those dreams, of course, were separated from reality by two hundred yards of field and the whims of a doe that had already been hounded by a smaller buck and now had to deal with this one.

Only a moment passed before the monster began bird-dogging the doe with just as much careless abandon as the younger buck displayed. *Only during the rut*, I thought as the doe made two quick circles in the field, matched step for step by the huge ten-pointer. A moment later, the doe dashed for a small wood lot to the west and the buck went along as if pulled on a string attached to her tail. Passing broadside at 175 yards, they disappeared into the timber. They were gone and there was not a thing I could do about it. Sitting in stony silence until dark, I prayed she would tire of that wood lot and move into mine. It never happened. I briefly considered moving the fallback stand up the list, past Pricker Pond, as the most frustrating place I've ever hunted, but I hadn't been there long enough to bestow upon it that distinction quite yet. The next morning, I quickly scouted the small wood lot and found the trail down which the doe had led the buck. Large white rubs on a dozen saplings lined the trail through the brush.

This year, only one single morning of gun season found me in that small wood lot, crouched inside a very small ground blind created from some wild grape vines. A small milk crate nestled into the center of the mess was my seat. There wasn't a suitable tree in the smaller lot, but there were many brush piles and tangles of vines, and my blind blended well enough with the background that two different squirrels walked across it only six inches from my back. It reminded me of my favorite blind in the Catskills from which I'd killed many of my deer, and at breathtakingly short ranges. To the south, my tree stand stood ignored in the opposite corner of the field. Before daylight, I'd shone my light on the buck trail just thirty yards from the stand and found it once again matted with fresh tracks in the snow. With several successes under my belt already this season, I didn't feel pressure to kill another deer, but neither could I keep the image of the big buck out of my mind as orange tendrils on the eastern horizon ignited the first few sparks of daylight. At that moment, I couldn't know that another day would pass in the fallback woods without a sighting. Had I been able to see the day's events, I probably wouldn't have mistaken the log for a bedded deer when the first rays of light pierced the woods. I would have known there would be no reason to remain motionless for the first hour until I dared reach for my binoculars, revealing the deer-shaped log and my own silliness. Had my crystal ball been working, I probably wouldn't have jumped out of my skin when a rabbit hopped out of the brush pile fifteen yards away. *He could have been a ten-pointer.* Had I known it would just be another quiet day in the fallback woods, I probably wouldn't have daydreamed about those high tines and those wide beams and wondered about the current price of whitetail taxidermy.

And what fun would that be?

28

THE GHOSTS THAT
WALK AMONG US

I CAN'T remember why Joy and I were walking the aisles of the big-box store in Niagara Falls. Maybe it was to stock up on gloves or batteries. Like eggs, milk, and bread on a grocery run during the off-season, gloves and batteries are staples during deer season. Maybe it was for a fresh bottle of deer pee, though that sounds somehow less important. It didn't matter when a ghost from my past walked right into us in aisle seven.

Cornered, with no escape from each other, I introduced Joy to my former hunting partner and friend. We'd long ago distanced ourselves from each other but there he was, larger than life. Together we'd walked miles of pheasant cover together and shot woodcock and pheasants and rabbits in numbers I couldn't even begin to calculate. *Hundreds.* Our friendship had blossomed within the shared passion of shooting upland along with the appreciation of the hardworking bird dogs that put us within shooting range of that game. He was one of my original hunting partners and many years had passed since I last saw his face. Our handshake in the cold florescent light of the big

chain store was hearty and strong and sad and, in the split second before I let his grip go, I felt happiness, sadness, remorse,
guilt, and a thousand other things. I don't know for certain but I
think he felt the same. After he'd said hello to Joy and then disappeared into the aisles of fish food and auto parts and cheap
foreign-made clothing, something hitched inside of me and I
could barely contain my sadness. We'd been fast friends, if only
when the dogs were working hard. No matter, we'd been good
friends at a time when those were not in great supply.

When my Maggie was only a pup he had purchased a can-
vas chest protector for her, alarmed at how beat up she was
after our pheasant and rabbit hunts. When Ted was just a babe
in the field, my old friend had directed him into the bird covers with a patience I didn't have. Ted always listened to him.
When it came to my first hunting crew of bird dogs, he was
their best friend and became a good friend of mine. If he was
good enough for my dogs, he was good enough for me. We
had worked together. Not just hunting work, but in real life. He
and I butted heads and were competitive and in the end were
willing players in office politics, a game from which winners
rarely emerge. During a particularly brutal head-cutting session, he was laid off while I retained my job. He cried in my
office while I celebrated silently, thankful that he would never
again terrorize my career. He and I would never again work
together, but that was not what haunted my thoughts. What
did haunt me was the knowledge that we'd never hunt together
again. Jobs come and go. Hunting partners should not. Unfortunately, they often do. Much like John and me in deer season,
during bird season my old friend and I had unwritten rules,
unspoken friendship, and understood many things that could
not and would not ever be said aloud. When I buried Maggie
and Ted at the back of the yard, I hadn't spoken to my old friend
in two years. I let him know of their passing in a short email.

Broken in spirit, I felt nothing but selfishness and felt I owed my former hunting partner and confidante nothing at all. Still, I chose to write him. No longer a fan of mine, nor even a friend, he acknowledged the loss with a brief email back that simply said, "I'm really sorry." There is no doubt in my mind that he was, and though the response might seem cold and impersonal to a passing observer, it was not. It was a small bridge across a huge ravine and differences aside, we both knew it. We haven't exchanged a word since. I hadn't expected to have any more communication with him, though, in my naïve hope for the best in people, I had hoped. Years passed. Nothing.

In those ten seconds when he gripped my hand in the cold light of the big box store, all those stories and all those years coursed like a lightning bolt between us. The feelings between us were hard, but the smile that flashed in the meeting of both of our eyes was not. It simply said, *I know.* On the way home, Joy gripped my hand as I grieved anew for Maggie and Ted and the friendships that would never live again. There's no more perfect time to remember the gray sorrow that inevitably accompanies the good things in life than the cold and harsh month of November. Summer and fall bow to its power and to its overwhelming sadness. November always wins.

29

RETURN TO THE LONELY RAVINE

THE RAVINE seemed lonelier today. Unlike opening day, there were no trucks on the long dirt road. No army of hunter orange lined the field edges like troops waiting for marching orders in the "Great Deer War." The boot tracks from the countless hunters that traversed the surrounding hills were nowhere to be seen, buried now under the unrelenting snow of the past few days. At the top of the ravine, just a few feet from where the opening-morning doe fell into the snow, I felt a sense of freedom and peace that I hadn't since squirrel season. The snow was six inches deeper now than it was just a week ago and walking was much more difficult than the day John and I dragged the big doe out. But it still looked like the deer woods in winter. The solitude had also returned to this deep drainage in southern New York. In that way, it more resembled September. The view different now, with the saplings stripped of their leaves and the sky, once hidden by a green canopy of sprawling beech and oak, exposed in all its gray, threatening doom. The warm blanket of leaves and ferns were hidden as well, painted over with a broad white brush. Settling into the nook of the many-trunked apple tree once again, I let my thoughts wander as the snow fell heavy and wet around me. No shots rang in the distance. The road was quiet. No trucks rumbled by on their way to deliver some bunch of hunters to a secret place that they knew to be better than any other.

I was alone.

I sat for an hour, long enough for my hunting clothes to become completely covered in snow. I felt even more a part of the lonely ravine, now fully assimilated. Though starting to soak through, I was completely hidden in the woods, and if a deer happened to notice me, it would be with their noses and not their eyes. Taking advantage of the white camouflage, I settled in for a second hour of motionless daydreaming. During a brief break in the heaviest snow, the squirrels emerged from their holes and leaf nests in the mature hardwoods around me. Three grays chased each other through the limbs of a towering oak. Down in the ravine I once again enjoyed the rare sight of a fox squirrel hopping through the snow. I couldn't tell if he was digging or burying, just that he was busy. He moved slowly, heavily, more like a rabbit than the slimmer, faster grays around me. This truly was squirrel paradise. I'd be back in September.

Daylight turned to morning, then mid-morning and the snow began again, this time taking its job a bit more seriously. Looking carefully around, I dusted off my clothes and my pack. I gathered up my rifle and began hiking down the ravine. With the number of hunters in the area on opening day, it would've been rude and rather pointless to move around much. With the mountain to myself, I looked forward to a slow stalk up the ravine if for no other reason than to warm up. For the first few hundred yards I walked slowly to bring up my body temperature. Once my blood began circulating again, I slowed and began *hunting*. Three or four steps at a time, I angled down the drainage along the dry creek, moving deeper and deeper into the ravine. Some of my best bucks have been taken while still-hunting, and I was well aware of the tendency for deer to lie still and allow hunters to pass. I examined each and every stump that seemed out of place, each and every horizontal line in the woods full of vertical lines. Every now and then, motion would cause a momentary hitch in my breath and heart rate, but each turned out to be a squirrel or a woodpecker or, in one case, a small mouse running up the side of an oak sapling just a few feet from me. As much as I enjoy stand hunting, there's nothing like the freedom of moving through the deer woods on your own schedule and trying to make things happen. There on the vast piece of public land, I would never cross a fence or an angry posted sign. Thousands of acres were waiting for me and I had the whole day to explore. With the memory still fresh of dragging the doe out of here and how hard it had been with two of us doing the work, I paralleled the road as much as possible without letting it dampen my spirit of exploration.

Only a half mile down the ravine, I whipped my head around as movement on the far side caught my attention. Three deer were moving high above me, angling downward into the dry creek bed. Remembering my amateur attempt to stealthily shed my gear at Nobleboro all those months ago (*was it really just last month?*), I didn't let the sighting throw me this time. With a week of deer hunting completed, I was somewhat reeducated in the practice of not making a fool of myself around deer. Emphasis on the *somewhat*.

When the does passed behind a snow-covered boulder, completely obscured from me, I shrugged the pack off my left shoulder and the rifle off of my right while crouching behind a beech sapling, the only cover I had available. Fifty yards from the next big clump of trees and twenty from the next boulder, I had no option other than to drop and get ready. The deer emerged from behind the boulder just as I leaned my rifle against the spindly beech trunk. Now a hundred yards from me, they were no longer coming directly down the ravine toward me, but turning, paralleling the dry creek bed on the opposite side, just forty yards above the bottom.

I flipped the scope covers up to verify that which I already knew. Does. Two does and a fawn. Having no more doe tags, I relaxed. Only for a moment. I turned my attention to their back trail, waiting for a buck. Waiting for *the* buck. Only scanning occasionally in their direction, I noticed the does had slowed considerably and were pawing for beechnuts and acorns in the creek bottom. When they turned abruptly and trotted up the steep bank on my side of the ravine, I was not surprised. The trees here were older. I remembered from squirrel season the forest floor in this small stretch had been so carpeted with fallen acorns that it was impossible to walk without crunching. The does fed within forty yards of me. I felt terribly exposed but had again become so covered with wet snow that my camouflage was nearly perfect in the white woods. Instead of continuing on down the ravine, the trio crossed into the brush between a large goldenrod field and the woods. I watched them go, pawing and feeding the whole way. Plumes of snow and oak leaves flew up as they hunted for treasure. That the deer were engaged in such leisurely feeding activities in the heart of a public hunting area during the first week of deer season was a surprise. *Then again*, I thought, *I'm the only one here.* They probably felt perfectly safe. I watched their back trail for a very long time, but no buck emerged. When they were long gone, I fumbled with cold hands through my pack to fetch a crushed and mutilated peanut butter sandwich that tasted almost as bad as it looked. My stomach had been rumbling so loudly that I thought the sound would give my location away to the does. I wolfed down the ugly sandwich.

With only one pair of dry gloves left, I decided I'd live with the *almost* dry pair for a while longer yet. Picking up the does' trail, feeling like a *real hunter*, I followed the tracks up and out of the ravine. They had crossed a small funnel at the edge of the large goldenrod field and passed into another unexplored patch of oak woods. From there I don't know where they went because I suddenly found myself in the Grand Central Station of deer activity. Though the snow was deep, acres and acres of the oak woods had been torn up, fresh orange and brown leaves lay atop the newly fallen snow. Tracks from what must have been at least two dozen deer crisscrossed the area. Deer droppings were as abundant as the acorn fragments scattered across the top of the snow. It was a deer wonderland. I don't ever recall seeing so many tracks in one place.

I wasn't quite sure what to do. It was obviously a place that deer were frequenting. Three different times I took up the fresh tracks of *groups* of deer only to find more acreage torn up and more evidence of recent feeding. The wise thing to do would be to sit down and wait the rest of the day. I did, however, want to explore the other places I hadn't yet seen to get a better feel for the land. *All this sign, though.* Compromising, I found another vast sea of oak leaves kicked onto fresh snow. I decided to sort out the tracks of one single group of deer and follow them wherever they went. The country was steep enough and the walking quiet enough in the deep snow that I knew I had a better-than-average chance of sneaking up on them. Selecting a set of tracks that appeared to number six or seven deer, I waited for a half hour and took up the tracks. They did not meander. A straight line ran from the hilltop feeding area to a low brush area in a ravine that I'd never before seen. An hour later I peeked over the top, only to see that they'd gone through the brush and up the other side—in a hurry. Their bounding tracks were staccato marks in the snow up the opposite bank.

I'm sure they heard me coming. I must have been right behind them. Knowing now that they'd be almost impossible to track, and running out of steam, I checked my compass and decided it was time to turn back toward the road. It would be nearly dark by the time I got out.

I crossed many more deer tracks, all of them fresher than today's snow, picking up a trail here and there only if it was headed northeast, back toward the road. It was easy to become complacent. Tracks covered the woods. I'd never seen so much sign in my entire life. Losing track of which ravine I was in, I again took my bearings with the compass, surprised I was still headed northeast. Snow fell more heavily now and there was no sun to help with the navigation. Feeling like a real woodsman, I didn't want to use the GPS. If darkness drew closer I might use the high-tech gadget. I figured I still had an hour or two and in that time I just wanted to enjoy the woods and maybe, just maybe, find some more deer.

The last ravine I descended ended not in a creek bottom but at a small lake. I was relieved. Darkness was not far off now and I recognized the lake and its two crooked wood duck boxes from my September hunting. The road wouldn't be far and I somehow had to get around the lake. To my right was deep woods and another ravine that I'd hunted for squirrels. To my left, the unknown.

I went left.

The choice seemed wise. The west end of the pond was cat-tail-choked and lined with dense brush. Deer tracks zigzagged in and out of the cover. Reminding me more of the flatlands than the wooded southern hills, the cover became increasingly dense. Soon I was slapping branches away and making more noise than one can make and still expect to see deer. I moved faster now, feeling the black encroachment of darkness and the knowledge that I had no idea what waited around the back side of the lake.

I fought my way through thornapples and twisted wild grapevines and multiflora rose that tore at my knit hat and more than once snagged my parka so tightly in its wicked grip that I had to violently twist myself free. Finally emerging from the cover, all that remained between the road and me was a thin strip of woods, and two wide-open fields. A pair of deer tracks intertwined on the open ice leading away from me and I wondered if I'd pushed them out of the cattails. Movement in the thin strip of brush drew my eye and, once again caught completely in the open, I crouched and slung my gear to the ground. A large brown shape moved through the thin strip of timber on the far side of the lake. I guessed the range to be about two hundred yards. Doable, but I'd be dragging in the dark. If it was a buck, dragging it out in the dark would be perfectly okay with me. The form stopped and turned in my direction. Slight wind gusts kicked a snowy mist up above the frozen lake between us, but I knew this wasn't a deer. Pulling the small binoculars out of my parka, I watched the young guy start in my direction, wearing his brown work coveralls and a black wool hat with a thin band of orange. Not the wisest apparel selection in a public deer hunting area, I thought, but his choice nonetheless. *Youth.* Emerging from the strip of timber, he spotted me. The conversation was brief and I did not lecture him on his choice of clothing during the busiest week of deer season. He was friendly to a stranger in a strange place, walking the right path in my book. I wanted to offer him my extra orange hat but talked myself out of it. Darkness fell as we walked silently out of the woods together. Of all the places on all of the roads that he could have parked and all the places he could have hunted on this exceptionally quiet day in deer country, he had parked right behind me.

30

VISITORS

WHEN I'M deer hunting, the squirrel hunting has never been better. When I'm carrying a gun there's never a shortage of wildlife photography that could have been shot. There are animals you are hunting and animals you are not hunting, and there is little doubt about which will be more plentiful during any given hunt.

When I bow hunted for the first time with Porter, he took a shot at a squirrel from one of my favorite deer stands, a fact that became apparent when he had to remove an arrow from a tree trunk when I came to pick him up. I used to be the ultimate opportunist, taking all kinds of small game during bow season from grouse to rabbits. While bird hunting, I've killed squirrels and raccoons and turkeys. I always laugh reading the advertisements for the latest and greatest turkey rounds with number-four shot plated with depleted uranium, or whatever is in fashion this year. I killed two of my best turkeys with light eight-shot and an open choke. Flushed during the late woodcock season, they hit the ground hard—if you've never seen a small springer spaniel retrieve a large turkey, put it on your list. I've killed foxes and coons while hunting for deer and a handful of coyotes as well. I'm still an opportunist but these days I tend to stick more closely to shooting what I'm after. It's not a hard and fast rule, but a guideline. The last raccoon I saw sunning himself in a high tree crotch during squirrel season would have been an easy shot with the twenty-two but I let him lounge. I'd like to tell myself that was because after almost three decades of hunting I've become more of a true sportsman. While that may be accurate, the deciding factor was probably more about having no desire to skin and/or carry out a dead raccoon.

In the past few years on the deer stand, I've watched foxes and coyotes, dozens of coons, countless red-tailed hawks, and a handful of horned owls. I've seen fishers and martins, weasels and mink and muskrats, and probably a handful of other beasts that I can no longer remember. When the furbearers are in season I'm no longer tempted to seize the moment for a trophy. However, not too long ago, a red fox spooked two bucks off and he very nearly became a wall decoration out of sheer frustration. The kinder and gentler sportsman I've become in recent years grudgingly let him walk. The animals that share the woods pass the time in a way that reading a paperback or surfing a smartphone cannot. I've told you about the squirrel wars at Pricker Pond. There are other regulars, too. The raccoons at the fallback stand across the road are a constant presence. Every night they creep around the stand just before dark. With their clumsy and bumbling gait, shuffling through the leaves for a nut here or an apple there before waddling down to the steelhead creek to fish for frogs and crayfish with their creepy human hands and shifty movements, they always look like they're about to steal something. Maybe it's the masks. A family of foxes lives there as well, though their visits are more sporadic. I've watched them out in the long-grass field, pouncing for mice as if catapulted. One night, a lone male fox caught several mice within fifty yards of the tree stand. Each time he caught one, he tossed it in the air with a shake of his head and then performed an acrobatic pounce to reacquire it. He played with his catch—*terrorized them*—much the same way a house cat does. Repeatedly throwing them around, he'd only stop when the fight went out of them and he had to catch a fresh one to keep it challenging. The hour spent watching the fox passed more quickly than any hour I've ever spent at that godforsaken, deer-less stand. It dawned on me later that having a carnivore playing around my stand would probably do little to increase the deer frequency in the area, but it was entertaining nonetheless.

Many years past the stage where I'm tempted to shoot whatever I'm allowed to shoot, I enjoy these visitors. I've had squirrels blow my cover when deer were nearby, but that hasn't happened in a long time. The reds are the worst culprits with their insect-like chatter and chirping, but the chipmunks also have a nasty habit of alerting every creature in the woods as if saying, "Hey, in case you guys didn't notice, there's a guy in that tree . . ." Blue jays, too. Don't get me started on blue jays. When there are no great horned owls or red-tailed hawks for the angry blue birds to harass, they are just as content making a human being's day miserable.

I've incorporated the squirrels and birds into my game. If I can remain hidden from them, I figure that I'm succeeding. In turn, wildlife activity around my stand becomes a natural camouflage, my way of saying, "Hey, look at all the birds and squirrels . . . no hunters here . . . no sir . . ."

Countless times while bear hunting, I've had young bears come and check me out. It would be a lie to say that having a black bear in your tree is much like having a gray squirrel in your tree. On my second Maine bear hunt, I was secluded in a large wooden ladder stand many miles from the road and many more miles from town. When the yearling bear wandered into sight and put his front paws on the bottom rungs of my ladder, I was amused—in a heart-palpitating kind of way. When he began to climb, the amusement quickly transformed into something different. While he never got closer than three feet from my boots, *he got three feet from my boots!!!* He was only a hundred-pound bear. That's not the point. He was a hundred-pound bear *on my stand!!!* Since that hunt, I've had other bears, even closer. You can't buy that kind of excitement.

Maine is a different planet than even the wilder places in New York. It is the Alaska of the northeast. There are plentiful bears and moose. More than once while bear hunting in Maine, a moose has walked by my stand. A moose walking by your stand is not like a big deer passing by. An adult moose is not a big deer, but a small mountain. Their movements seem slow and deliberate but if, in your excitement to get your camera out of your pack, you happen to startle one at ten yards? Let's just say that one of you will run away, snapping every sapling in your path while the other participant suffers severe enough shock that it will be difficult to focus for the rest of the afternoon.

Most of the visitors I've known aren't so dramatic. They go on about their lives, not much interested in the two hundred pounds of camouflage that preposterously assumes he's well hidden on a bare poplar trunk sixteen feet off the ground. They hunt and gather without much thought to human intrusion. I've learned much more from watching the wild creatures of the woods than I have by surfing Wikipedia. Time used to pass slowly on the stand. It no longer does. Immersing myself into that which is going on around me, right here, right now, *this very moment,* has been a lesson learned over many long seasons.

Maybe I'm finally catching on.

31

THE NEW PLACE

THERE'S SOMETHING wonderful about someplace new.

New hunting grounds are unexplored and uncharted. While it might not be untamed, it is at the very least *unknown*. There hasn't been enough time for it to become a bad-luck place like Pricker Pond. On the other hand, there hasn't been enough good luck to put it on the roster of "Great Places to Hunt" that exists in every big-game hunter's mind. Memories are not yet rich enough for it to rise to the level of, say, Nobleboro Bridge. My brother-in-law Steve has been one of my longtime hunting partners. While he normally hunts somewhere other than with me for opening week of deer season, he also spent many years with me in the hallowed Catskill deer woods during opening week. Still, it's been a long time since we've hunted together for deer. I'd put my time in with John in the southern hills and I'd hunted hard around home in the difficult and promising terrain of the Lake Ontario rim. I had not yet, however, hunted Steve's latest piece of property. I agreed to hunt the land in a new county, in a part of the state with which I had no familiarity. Even if my brother-in-law and nephew Eric were not going, I wouldn't have rejected the invitation. I enjoy hunting new places. I like to explore. When there's no history of bad luck, it's hard to have premonitions and doubts about how badly the day will go, unless you're the worst kind of pessimist. When it comes to hunting, that I am not.

Our first trip to the mountains of West Almond, New York, passed without incident. Well, not exactly *without incident*, but no one killed a deer. The weather was wet and snowy and cold. Steve had provided a rudimentary map, complete with GPS coordinates, and for the first few hours I dutifully sat in the places where he had marked deer sign and deer trails and deer sightings. After lunch and almost no deer activity, I set out on my own. Left to my own devices and my own imagination, a mountaintop pond was the first landmark I discovered. The pond, a natural diversion in the woods, was surrounded with deer beds and fresh trails, rubs, and every other kind of deer sign you can imagine. I'd only just begun to explore the pond when a deer jumped from a bed concealed in a tangle of blackberry bushes. A hundred yards farther, I was looking down and following tracks when I glanced to my left and saw a huge doe. Knowing that the place had not been hunted in years, I was no less shocked to see her studying me at less than fifty yards. If I'd had a doe tag, the rest of the afternoon would have been spent dragging her out.

I didn't.

On that first trip, we met at the truck for lunch. I had still-hunted, tracked, and sat. I saw deer at every turn. Eight in total. All does. Eric and Steve had seen a combined total of no deer. *Zero.* It was hard not to tell my stories of close encounters and plentiful deer. Lunch was remarkably quiet. At one point I did tell Eric he should think about wearing some more hunter orange, thinking about the kid in the southern tier as I was met with a silent nod. I didn't mind.

The other kid wasn't my nephew.

A few weeks later we went back. This time making a direct line for the lower portion of the pond that had taken me all morning to find last time, it was hard to relax. The sign was again plentiful, the woods quiet and welcoming, but my nerves had not quite recovered from our road trip. The narrow dirt track from the highway up to Steve's friend's cabin this time was slick with ice, exacerbated and lubricated by a few hours of freezing rain just before we arrived. The truck bucked and slid and threatened to go off into the woods a dozen times. Steve is a good driver, but there were several moments that I was tempted to either grab the wheel or bail out the passenger-side door. It was a glaze of ice and we were miles from help if something happened. There were no other tracks on the rutted path, though we did see gouges in the snow and mud where someone had tried to make it out before skidding off the hill and into the woods. Everyone's nerves were shot. When we located the gate to the cabin in the hazy, rainy gauze of pre-daylight, the trip was far from over. Steve pulled the SUV off the side of the road and we both slipped and slid. Steve took a hard fall trying to cross the road to unlock the metal gate. Seeing his tumble, I opened my door to help him and promptly went onto my ass as well. The freezing rain kept coming. It was miserable. Before the hunt even started, the three of us were wet, cold, and not at all focused on the task at hand.

In an attempt to be a good uncle and a responsible hunting partner, I gave Eric my old blaze-orange vest, since I'd gotten a new version as a Christmas present. Much to his boredom, I'd passed along the stories of the various deer that had fallen to the good luck instilled in that faded orange garment, and at one point called it my "Lucky Vest." Even if he didn't appreciate the stories, he put it on.

Steve and Eric went east, while I angled west toward the funnel on the downslope side of the pond where I'd seen so much activity last time. Finding a small hollow in the brook below the pond, I dug in and cleared the leaves at the base of a large hemlock. A slight breeze kicked up and drove the freezing rain into every seam and zipper of every hunting garment I owned. The day was not fit for man nor beast. Early on, I caught a glimpse of a small deer picking its way through the multiflora rose in the brook bottom, seeking cover from the deluge. Watching it for a moment through binoculars that long ago fogged over from the cold moisture, I verified it was a doe before hiding once again in the depths of my hunting gear. Thirsty from the long walk in, I didn't want to dig for the water bottle in the bottom of my pack, worried that I'd soak the rest of the contents in my effort to retrieve it. I wondered about Eric and Steve. I've killed some good bucks on wet, hopeless days, but we were all worried about how we were going to get back out on the treacherous icy track back to the main road. The thought gnawed at me all morning, sucking some of the life from the morning hunt.

We'd agreed to meet at eleven. Sometime before then (it was too wet to check my cell without ruining it) I was about to rise from my hideout at the base of the great hemlock to stretch and shake some water off when movement caught my eye. A very small doe appeared fifty yards from me. If it had been a better day and my head had been on a swivel, as it usually is while deer hunting, I may have spotted the deer when it was still far enough out to do something. With the intense freezing rain and unbearable conditions, I'd withdrawn into the deep collar of my parka, intent only on the woods in front of me and oblivious to what was happening behind me.

Behind me is where the deer appeared.

Water dripped down my neck as I quickly craned around to get a better look. The small deer was one of four. Moving quietly through the wet, snowy woods, two does and two fawns were within spitting distance before I even saw them. I'd been perfectly still and they had no idea that I was there. With no doe tags, I carefully checked their back trail as they approached to twenty yards, then fifteen, and then ten.

Just when it looked like they were going to step on me, I spotted the buck.

Fifty yards behind the group of does and fawns, he was not spectacular. His four or five points made up a set of antlers the likes of which I'd shot a great number during my early years of hunting. Still, I was excited. The light rack stood out in stark contrast against the dark hemlocks. My heart pounded and my grip tightened on the rifle. There was no doubt that, given the opportunity, I would shoot this buck. Closing the distance to forty yards, the buck stopped behind a large hemlock. Covered in rain and concealed in the shadows, his coat looked black. I needed to pivot slightly to get in position to shoot, but the does were still too close. With more hemlocks to block my movements, I let the does and fawns pass before attempting to line up for the shot. The quartet of deer, now at point-blank range, passed my exposed position without so much as a suspicious glance. Realizing I'd been holding my breath, I let it out slowly as the last of the four deer passed only ten yards from me and into the brush to the west near the pond. I stole a glance at the buck, now only twenty-five yards away. Quietly spinning on my seat, I propped the Winchester on my knee and snicked the safety off. Perfectly hidden behind one last tree, whether he stepped forward or turned back to flee all I had to do was shoot. My breathing was ragged but calmed as I waited.

To my right one of the does suddenly blew a warning snort. I snapped my head reflexively in her direction and she saw the movement. Though safely past me, she'd either scented me or caught my movement in her peripheral vision. The four deer were locked in place. The last and largest doe stared in my direction before finally stomping her hoof. I'd blown it. Quickly shifting my attention back to the buck, ready to shoot the moment he emerged from behind the dark-brown trunk of the hemlock, I was heartbroken to see him already rocketing off into the woods, his white tail bobbing through the dark timber. Though the does were still close, I quickly stood and popped the covers off my scope, finding the buck. With my finger inside the trigger guard I waited for any pause in his flight. He didn't pause. He never slowed. The moment never came. He was gone, vanishing over the ridge as quickly as he had appeared. The fawns and does, fully alerted to my location, blasted off in the other direction, blowing angry warnings as they went. I sat back down at the base of the hemlock and ate a wet sandwich. At times like those, there's not much else to do. It was the closest I'd been to killing a buck all gun season and it was over before it had even begun.

Back at the truck, Steve was soaked and shivering. Eric, who had taken up temporary shelter under the cabin, was only slightly better off.

"Lucky vest," he said, rolling his eyes.

"Did you see anything?" I asked.

Once again, they had not. I debated not telling them my story this time, fairly certain that it wouldn't be appreciated. In the end, I told them.

They were polite about it.

32

THE GHOSTS OF PRICKER POND: PART III—GOODBYE

I'VE TOLD you stories about Pricker Pond but there's something I haven't yet shared. You know that it is one of the most hard-luck places I've ever hunted. I've killed a handful of deer at a nearby stand, but never at the pond—not until this year when I shot the doe at sunset on opening night. I knew then that would likely be my first and last. It isn't the lack of luck that will prevent me from hunting the property around Pricker Pond. If the decision were up to me, I'd be hunting and bitching about hunting the place for years to come. I've become attached to Pricker Pond in a self-inflicted kind of way.

The sad truth is that I'll probably never hunt there again.

The stand at Pricker Pond and the other stand to the east are part of a parcel of property belonging to an old friend of mine. He just retired and is fleeing south to escape the frigid winters. I can't blame him, and before this deer season even began, I knew it would likely be the last year I could complain about my luck at Pricker Pond.

I've lost hunting property over the years. Like the cycles of nature, these things ebb and flow. There are places I can no longer hunt for which I have truly grieved. In some ways, losing the stand at Pricker Pond is even harder. Finally scoring on a deer after dozens of failures didn't help ease the blow. Maybe the doe was my parting gift from the ghosts of Pricker Pond. This weighed heavily on my mind the evening I dragged her out. Since that day I've thought more than once how it would likely be the first and last deer I would ever drag out of that miserable thicket. The finality of the thought didn't discourage me.

It may have inspired me to hunt even harder.

Far too cold to sit still, the third week of deer season found me high above the thicket overlooking the alliterative pond. The dawning light was blinding—the reason I never hunt the stand in the morning. With other plans for the evening and a disagreeable wind at the stand that I would have preferred to hunt, I enjoyed Pricker Pond's familiar surroundings. Now late in the season, I tried to absorb the scenery and live in the moment, knowing this was the last time I would hunt here. Sometime in the spring I would need to return to take down my stands but that's just a chore and not at all the same thing as *hunting* a place. Nature unfortunately rewarded me with a deep freeze. I suspected the cold might get the deer moving but, being Pricker Pond, that was an overly optimistic view of a highly unlikely scenario. At eight-thirty, no longer able to feel my hands or feet, I climbed down. Stepping off the ladder at the base of the tree, my feet thudded to the ground. They were so numb that I looked down to make sure I was not just standing on broken, icy stumps.

In the woods and thickets around the pond, old trails zigzag and loop through the heaviest cover. With hunting pressure on, the deer hold tight in these impenetrable bedding areas, often allowing a hunter to walk right past before bolting for cover. It's not an ideal place for a still-hunt but I needed to move and get my circulation going. Reloading the revolver, barely able to feel the stubby brass shells with my frozen fingers, I picked a point at the farthest part of the property and began walking. I covered the ground briskly at first; I needed to warm up. Nearing the thicket, though, I slowed as I approached. Through the sea of twigs and vines and saplings, I kept a sharp eye for any horizontal line that might be a bedded deer. Hoof prints in and out of the cover were imprinted on the fresh snow. I was on the right track, but after circling the two-acre thicket, I decided I'd either pushed the deer out the far side, or the tracks were made earlier in the morning.

Circling back toward the pond and woods and finally warm enough to function at least on a rudimentary level, I slowed my pace. One step, then two, then pause. Repeat. I crept slowly into the woods, placing my feet carefully, wary of any dark shape in the white landscape of saplings and willow trees. Even the squirrels were absent in the frigid air. My breath escaped in clouds of steam and I noticed the faint breeze that had accompanied daylight was gone. The morning was still. Ice crystals illuminated by the rising sun made the thick woods even more impenetrable from the blinding brightness. The snow, usually a quieting factor, was frozen and squeaked like angry rodents under my feet. Under these conditions it would be nearly impossible to stalk up on a deer. I moved carefully through the woods, passing the ladder stand before looping back around to the pond. After stalking around the backside of Pricker Pond, I moved up along the goose field. Tracks littered the area, some of them within fifty yards of my deer stand. With that amount of sign, I should have seen deer every day. The place was thick with their tracks.

Ghosts.

Tracing a single set of larger tracks, I followed them into the thicket below my stand. They eventually led to a tunnel in the brush so dense that I'd have had to crawl on my hands and knees to follow. I briefly considered it before turning back toward the pond to gather the backpack I'd left hanging on the ladder. A glint of white against a dark trunk caught my eye and I suddenly remembered the skull. Wedged between the wild grapevines and a honeysuckle trunk, it was exactly as I'd left it the night John and I tracked my buck through this same thicket. I'd forgotten about it. Prying it loose with cold fingers I tucked the big doe skull, smooth and white as a museum specimen, under my arm.

I haven't been back to Pricker Pond since. Once the weather warms (which right now in the heart of February seems an awfully long way off), I'll pick up the stands and take one long, last look around, but it won't be the same as hunting. For now, the doe skull has taken up residence next to some other mementos on the hearth. Like so many of the other antlers and skulls that hold some significance for me deep in their weathered bone, this one does as well.

She's the last ghost of Pricker Pond.

33

THE FUTURE

Don't judge each day by the harvest that you reap but by the seeds that you plant.

—Robert Louis Stevenson

LIKE THE cycles of nature, the world moves on. Eventually we all pass into the next realm. The Augusts and Septembers of our lives turn to autumn, then winter and then we are gone. Spending time in the outdoors reminds me of that truth. Sometimes it's a comfort to know that we're bound by the same rules as the creatures of the woods. Sometimes the future and what lies beyond is fearful. It's human nature to want to leave some reminder of ourselves. Many of my ghosts of autumn, those who inspired me but have since moved on, were wonderful people. I try to honor them, but it's not easy to keep another's memory alive when you're busy with the fulltime job of living. When I fail at trying, I go to the woods and picture their faces and try to remember their voices. With the frigid air and lonely quiet of the deep woods, remembering is effortless. Mostly what I remember about my outdoor mentors was their eagerness to pass on their passions, and the patience to make sure that I got it right. I'm not much for copying the actions of others, but that trait is one that I strive to emulate.

In that regard, this year has been a success.

The first big-game hunt of the year at Nobleboro Bridge brought me the warm certainty that the torch has been passed on to Porter, my skilled young hunting partner and nephew. Later on in the season, I was thrilled to get the text that my other nephew, Eric, had killed his first deer, complete with photos from my brother-in-law Steve. I remembered getting Steve started deer hunting, recalling the day with crystal clarity when Steve shot his first deer, a small button buck. I was far younger and perhaps a bit more cruel. John and I suggested that, for the photo session, Steve tuck the little buck's legs underneath to "puff him up." All it served to do was make the small deer look smaller. Each year after, we'd laugh about Steve's trophy photos. Steve always responded the same way: *"Bastards."* Those were fun days and the memories are still treasures of a time now twenty-some-odd years gone. I can't begin to tell you how glad I am that he has passed the deer-hunting torch down to Eric. Ice storm and all, my time at the "New Place" with them this fall felt as if it was just another small piece of the puzzle that eventually forms a full circle.

Hunting season was already mostly over when Joy's cousin Vicky asked me to mentor her daughter, Ashley, and take her hunting. With my own daughters grown now, I didn't have much current experience in the ways of teenage girls, but figured that things probably haven't changed that much in the last ten years or so since I lived with two of them. Honored to be asked, I agreed without hesitation. Making contact on social media (how else?), Ashley and I agreed on a trip or two to the local squirrel-hunting woods.

The first hunt was a bust for squirrels but a success nonethe-less. Walking for miles through the open woods near the lake where, not coincidentally, I started this hunting season (as well as this book), we walked and talked and talked and talked. She wanted to know about my bear hunts and wanted to share how she started hunting with her dad when she was four. He's been gone a few years now and the pain is still *right there*. More than once a lump formed in my throat as she told stories in that matter-of-fact way kids have that tends to slice through the bullshit. Silence between us was punctuated by the crunching of snow and frozen oak leaves underfoot. It was a good talk. Three times squirrels crossed our path, assuming we weren't serious about killing them. Maybe we weren't. That was the get-to-know-you hunt and by the time we arrived back at the truck, just in the nick of darkness, we'd gotten to know each other.

Our next hunt was different. On our first outing, we'd discov-ered a patch of white oaks that had been recently made acces-sible thanks to a newly opened trail through a nasty thicket. It was there that we encountered two of the three squirrels and I mentally marked the spot for the next hunt. This hunt.

Ashley's face was beet-red from the biting cold after the long hike into the oak woods. "Doing okay?" I asked.

"Yep." She was quiet today, almost a different kid.

Once in the woods, movement in the ancient oak tops imme-diately caught our attention. Three gray squirrels were chas-ing each other in the tree above us, oblivious to our presence. I hung back and motioned Ashley to move in. In a moment, twenty-two shots cracked in the quiet woods. The squirrels scattered, one of them perching just above me. I didn't shoot, hoping Ashley would see it. She didn't because she was already creeping up on another tree. More shots. No squirrels. At her third volley, one of the squirrels raced across a thick branch before flinging itself onto the thick trunk of an old maple. I couldn't resist. The squirrel tumbled sixty feet to the ground. Although I was only a dozen yards from the tree, I couldn't find it. With the soft carpet of leaves and almost a foot of snow, it had been swallowed up upon reentry. Ashley watched me quizzically as if wondering how I could possibly have lost it. I wondered the same thing. Finally, a small blood drop on a branch and a tiny clump of hair in the snow solved the mystery. I pulled the squirrel out of the hole—just a small gray—and held it up. Ashley, already stalking another squirrel, turned and gave me a quick thumbs-up.

I wasn't paying attention when she shot again. The woods erupted in squirrels. At least seven of them raced through the treetops. When two paused on a trunk large enough to make a safe backstop, I fired, missing miserably. Somewhere in the back of my consciousness, I vaguely remember Ashley shooting again. I've never seen so many squirrels in one place. Five minutes didn't pass between sightings and, usually, far less at that. Probably untouched for years, this place was a honeyhole. I'm glad my new hunting partner came along to discover it with me.

We paralleled each other through the woods until the activity died down. With a wary eye on the sun, now low in the western horizon, I spotted something out of place high in the crotch of an oak. It was another squirrel, trying very hard to be invisible. I called Ashley over and pointed at it until she spotted it. Raising her rifle, she missed. When it paused on the next tree, I did the same. Ashley cast a sideways glance at me that simply said, *We suck.* It was a fun moment. We were still only a few yards apart when a squirrel skittered down an oak trunk, pausing only yards from us. Ashley planted her feet and pulled the trigger on her twenty-two. Nothing happened. The squirrel waited patiently.

"*It's jammed,*" she whispered. I took the rifle from her and noticed the chamber was open.

"It's empty."

Embarrassed, she uttered a few words that surprised me.

She felt a little better when I told her that I'd left my extra magazine in the truck and the sad truth was I'd burned through five of my seven shots with only one squirrel to show for it. I didn't feel better admitting to my young apprentice that I didn't remember the basic rule of bringing plenty of ammunition. By the time we regrouped from the latest misadventure in an afternoon full of them, it was nearing dark and the walk back to the truck was not inconsiderable. There was some small talk and I made a point of telling her that the amount of squirrel activity was far more than we could have hoped for. Before we'd gone a hundred yards though, we again fell into silence. I was worried that she was upset about all the missed shots—or something else.

"You're not talking much, today," I said.

"No. Not really."

With that, my assumption that teenage girls haven't changed that much in the past decade was proven correct. Nearing the road in the glowing twilight, the conversation picked back up again. As we got into the truck, Ashley thanked me for a fun afternoon. I assured her it had been for me, as well.

That is how our light stays lit after we are gone. This is how the circle continues.

34

THE SURVIVORS

BACK AT the farm where I learned to pick tomatoes and tell dirty jokes and to find something fun in every day, I huddled in for the last hour of deer season. Late from work on this important milestone in hunting season, I wouldn't have time to get cold before it became too dark to hunt. Crouched over my muzzleloader, I thought to the winter ahead. Before long it would be time to start writing. I had a few ideas. For now, deep in the heart of December, the snow fell quietly around me as the evening grew darker, as much from the clouds as from the dwindling of the daylight.

There was no last-minute reprieve. No flickering ear betrayed the presence of a hidden deer. No dark shapes materialized from the lonely recesses of the wood lot. When darkness fell, it was over. Deer season came to a close with a fresh carpet of snow and the knowledge that I'd hunted as hard as I could for as long as I could, right up to the last minute. As much as I'd miss deer season, I was ready for a break. Climbing down, I avoided the third step from the bottom with its creaky, metallic clank. I supposed it didn't matter now.

Cars passed on the busy country road, oblivious to the tired hunter emerging from woods under the cover of darkness. Cold bit at my ears and face as I wiped the rifle down and slipped it into its case for the short ride home. I shed layers of clothes in the dark, tossing them into the back of the truck with none of the care I'd used the rest of the season. I'd sort them out tomorrow.

Or whenever.

Turning the key to warm the truck enough to get the ice off the windows, I stood by the side of the truck in the dark taking one last look over the bean field. Three dark shapes moved near the back of the field. Deer. I didn't bother digging for my binoculars. I could see them well enough with the snowy backdrop, even in the dark. Wondering if they were the same three that Joy had seen on her way to work in the summer, I decided that they probably were. Only a hundred yards from me, they seemed to know that the season had come to a close. They'd managed to make it through hunting season and now had only to worry about surviving the winter before the harsh weather again gave way to the warmth of spring and the cycle of life began anew. It would be here in a few short months, and the harshness of November and December would fade into a cold, harmless memory. I watched till their shapes blended in with the shadows and the last ghosts of autumn became one with the encroaching darkness.

35

EPILOGUE:
THE GHOSTS OF WINTER

WRITING A book about the people, dogs, wild animals, and activities you love—even the strangers you've encountered who've made some mark on your memory—is not a difficult task. To paraphrase another writer, all you have to do is sit down at the computer and bleed. As long as I've been hunting, I've been writing about hunting and sharing the stories with people I don't know. Some of those people have reached across the void between writer and reader and some have become my friends. I hope that others read these words and these stories and just say, "Yeah, I've been there. I've felt that." That to me is the wildest success. There is nothing better.

This is the Lascaux of my memories and I'm glad you found it. If you've read the stories of this past autumn and enjoyed them, you are also one of my ghosts of autumn. I know you're out there. Maybe I'll see you one day out in the fields and we'll talk for a bit while our dogs compare notes and smell each other's smelly places.

Max is looking out the window into the dark, hoping the rabbit that haunts our bird feeder will make an appearance. There's not much for a bird dog to do in February. Looking remarkably like the little dog that broke my heart, Lucy is curled up on the floor, maybe dreaming her own dreams of chasing birds and breathing the fresh air of autumn, running free as the wind in her new life.

I'm living in the little farm town where I grew up, in the house that used to be my grandmother's. I have been typing at the old library table that used to be my great-grandmother's. The girl I dreamed of when I was just a little boy in this little town is on the couch just a few feet away, patiently waiting for me to emerge from a winter entirely spent writing—one that came right on the heels of an autumn entirely spent hunting. Joy is patient.

The ghosts are always with me. I don't let them haunt my future. The ghosts of autumn—of my life—are all around me. They encourage me. When I quiet my mind and take a moment to listen to those who have moved on, they remind me to live while the living is good. This journey called life might seem long at times but, like a good bird field or a lonely patch of deer woods, it doesn't go on forever.

Outside, the wind is pushing drifts of February snow across the driveway and it's a long time until hunting season rolls around again.

Until then, my friends.

Joel Spring
January 1, 2015–February 17, 2015